# WAR'S OFFENSIVE ON WOMEN

## The Humanitarian Challenge in Bosnia, Kosovo, and Afghanistan

### Julie A. Mertus

with a case study by Judy A. Benjamin

for the Humanitarianism and War Project

KUMARIAN
PRESS

*War's Offensive on Women:*
*The Humanitarian Challenge in Bosnia, Kosovo, and Afghanistan*

Published 2000 in the United States of America by Kumarian Press, Inc.,
1294 Blue Hills Avenue, Bloomfield, Connecticut 06002 USA.

The UK Department for International Development (DFID) supports
policies, programmes, and projects to promote international development.
DFID provided funds for this study as part of that objective but the views
and opinions expressed are those of the author alone.

*Production and design by Nicholas A. Kosar.*
*Proofread by Jody El-Assadi. Index by Barbara J. DeGennaro.*
*The text of this book is set in 10/13 Adobe Sabon.*

Printed in Canada on acid-free paper by
Transcontinental Printing and Graphics, Inc.
Text printed with vegetable oil-based ink.

∞ The paper used in this publication meets the minimum requirements
of the American National Standard for Information Sciences—Permanence of
Paper for Printed Library Materials, ANSI Z39.48–1984.

**Library of Congress Cataloging-in-Publication Data**
Mertus, Julie, 1963–
   War's offensive on women : the humanitarian challenge in Bosnia,
Kosovo, and Afghanistan / Julie A. Mertus ; with a case study on Afghanistan
by Judy A. Benjamin.
     p.     cm.
   "For the Humanitarianism and War Project".
   Includes bibliographical references and index.
   ISBN 1–56549–118–1 (cloth : alk. paper). — ISBN 1–56549–117–3
(pbk. : alk. paper)
   1. War relief. 2. Women—Crimes against. 3. Women and war—History—20th century. 4. Yugoslav War, 1991–1995—Women. 5.
Women—Afghanistan. [1. Kosovo (Serbia)—History—Civil War, 1998—
Women.] I. Benjamin, Judy A. II. Title.

   HV639 .M47 2000
   362.87'082—dc21
                                              00–056833

09 08 07 06 05 04 03 02 01 00      10 9 8 7 6 5 4 3 2 1

First Printing 2000

# CONTENTS

# FOREWORD

THE FIRST DECADE in the post–Cold War era has represented a wake-up call for persons and institutions committed to humane values.

The list of major emergencies from the 1990s is a long one. It includes Kurds displaced on the northern border of Iraq; genocide and its aftermath in Cambodia and Rwanda, widespread famine in Somalia; all manner of suffering in the Balkans, from Croatia and Bosnia early in the decade through Kosovo at its end; displacement in the north and south Caucasus; and post-election pillage in East Timor. Crises in some areas—Afghanistan, the Sudan, and Liberia are examples—have spanned the entire decade.

Many such post–Cold War conflicts have been characterized by, and rooted in, egregious violations of fundamental human rights. Humanitarian agencies accustomed to delivering food, health care, shelter, and other life-sustaining resources have been challenged to address the reality that the civilians they seek to assist are not incidental victims of violence but often the specific target of military and political strategies.

This is certainly true of civilian populations as a whole. It is also true of women and girls within these populations. In wartime, women may be victims of sexual abuse and other forms of torture. They are often also subjected to forced displacement, arbitrary internment, and summary execution. It is often women who have to shoulder increased responsibility for families after men have gone off to war. Pregnant and nursing women are particularly vulnerable to lack of food and health care.

Yet women are more than passive victims of violence. They are also actors in their own right. The experience of dislocation and life in refugee or resettlement camps can be a mobilizing experience. The forging of alliances of war-affected women within their countries and with networks in the wider world have been forces for reducing the destructiveness of war and tackling the deeply rooted inequities in power relations that have sparked such conflicts. The process of humanitarian action, sensitively managed, can itself be empowering.

This book is about war and its impacts, positive and negative alike, on women. It is about understanding more clearly the dynamics of such conflict. It seeks to sensitize humanitarian organizations, and the broader community of policymakers, academics, and the concerned international public, to the challenges that conflict poses. It highlights the evolving international legal framework that protects human rights, including the rights of women, and that provides a vehicle for greater accountability.

The fact that all three countries highlighted in this volume have involved crises with large Muslim populations is something of a coincidence. As noted throughout, gender problems exist in all geographical areas and pose challenges in all crises. Indeed, differences are observed in the forms those challenges take even among the three countries reviewed.

The book is one in a series published by the Humanitarianism and War Project, an independent policy research initiative that has closely monitored developments during the first post–Cold War decade. Using an inductive method based primarily on interviews with those involved in the conflicts—relief and human rights personnel, local and national government officials, the media, and ordinary citizens—the Project has conducted a series of country and thematic studies of the dynamics of humanitarian action. It has made recommendations to organizations seeking to respond to such conflicts.

Founded in 1991 and based since 1994 at Brown University's Thomas J. Watson Jr. Institute for International Studies, the Project moved in September 2000 to the Feinstein International Famine Center at Tufts University's School of Nutrition and Science Policy in Medford, Massachusetts. It is supported by funds contributed by humanitarian organizations, governments, and foundations.

This book is one in a series of research publications by the Project. Others of particular relevance to human rights and gender issues are *A Humanitarian Practitioner's Guide to International Human Rights Law*, by William G. O'Neill, and *Protecting Human Rights: The Challenge to Humanitarian Organizations*, by Mark Frohardt, Diane Paul, and Larry Minear. A third study draws on the experience of the United Nations in integrating human rights in its humanitarian work, *When Needs Are Rights: An Overview of UN Efforts to Integrate Human Rights in Humanitarian Action*, by Karen Kenny. These and other resources are listed in the bibliography.

Our review of gender issues is part of a wider examination during

Phase 3 of the Project of the intersections between human rights and emergency assistance, undertaken with the encouragement and financial support of The Andrew W. Mellon Foundation, The Ford Foundation, and the Netherlands Foreign Ministry. A more detailed description of the Project is found at the back of the book. Additional information, including a complete list of contributors and publications, is available at the Project's website, www.hwproject.tufts.edu.

This particular study was made possible in part through a grant from the United Kingdom Department for International Development (DfID), which has had a special interest both in gender issues and in the countries reviewed. DfID is the government agency that manages British contributions to international humanitarian and development programs. It works with multilateral and nongovernmental organizations as well as mounting its own bilateral initiatives. We appreciate its support.

We are particularly pleased to have enlisted Julie A. Mertus as author of the present volume. She is a professor of international human rights law with a specialty in gender issues. The case studies on Bosnia and Kosovo reflect her field research. The case study on Afghanistan was contributed by Judy A. Benjamin, also based on her experience over the past decade. Both women have served as consultants on gender and human rights issues to a wide range of practitioner organizations and have written extensively on these issues. We wish to express particular appreciation to the Women's Commission for Refugee Women and Children, which commissioned much of the field research on which they have drawn. Further biographical information is provided in the About the Authors section at the back of this book.

We also wish to express appreciation to Judith A. Mayotte, who read the manuscript in draft form and contributed many helpful suggestions. Katherine Guernsey of the Pettit College of Law at Ohio Northern University also provided research assistance. We are also grateful to Watson Institute staff who have assisted at various points in the process: Margareta Levitsky, Ryoko Saito, and Laura Sadovnikoff. Special thanks go to the developmental editor of this book, Mary Lhowe.

Larry Minear, Director
Humanitarianism and War Project

# PREFACE

WAR HAS LONG BEEN an offensive against women. Today more than ever, women and children are the casualties of deliberate and systematic violence against entire populations. However, women are not just the victims of combat and the beneficiaries of humanitarian efforts. They are also the engines of resistance and key problem solvers in their communities. This book examines new ways in which citizens in areas of conflict, humanitarian organizations, and international legal processes respond to and moderate the impact of war on women. In particular, the study analyzes efforts to meet the humanitarian challenge of protecting and assisting women in emergency aid and postconflict reconstruction settings. Special attention is given to recent experience in such places as Bosnia, Kosovo, and Afghanistan.

To some extent, there has been great progress in the ways humanitarian organizations respond to women's needs and take cues from them in charting their course in crafting solutions. One of the most important changes has been the adoption by many aid groups of a gender perspective. Such a perspective takes into account how the different roles, opportunities, and constraints of men and women influence their needs in times of humanitarian crisis. By contrast, the earlier approach to enhancing the role of women, characterized as "add woman and stir," reflected a desire to solve "women's" problems by creating "special" women's programs for their "special" needs. This earlier approach simply substituted women for men in agency staffs and beneficiary communities without making space for the insights that women bring to solving humanitarian problems and without addressing imbalances in power relations. A gender perspective emphasizes using the expertise of women and including women in central decision-making processes in all stages and aspects of humanitarian action. It promises transformative change by examining the socially constructed roles of men and women and exposing the very root of exploitation and domination of women. It challenges the institutions that perpetuate inequality.

The World Conference on Women in Beijing in 1995 catapulted gender issues to the world stage. For humanitarian organizations, this new awareness resulted in a flurry of policy statements and programmatic changes, all with the avowed desire to integrate gender concerns throughout their work. These changes, however, rarely lead to transformative institutional change. While some organizations did examine their own management practices, most of the changes targeted overseas activities. And despite well-honed gender policy statements at headquarters and the expressed desire for improved programs, those activities continued to approach gender unevenly.

The lack of more wide-ranging change was in part gender-related and in part inherent in the nature of humanitarian work. Humanitarian organizations, by design, resist top-down change. Many agencies, particularly as a result of changes in recent years, tend to be decentralized, with projects driven more by strong personalities in the field than by headquarters mandates. When staff wish to work on gender problems, they do; when they do not, they find some reason to steer clear of gender. They often justify resistance to taking on gender concerns as "Western issues" that have nothing to do with the populations in need. The emergency nature of many relief operations—the "tyranny of the emergency"—also deprioritizes gender issues. Even if some staff enthusiastically face up to gender issues, their organizations may not back them up with serious institutional commitments that outlast rapid personnel turnover. Although some agencies have developed more long-lived institutional tools for tackling gender issues, many more have not. In addition, the results-oriented nature of humanitarian aid penalizes gender projects, as improvements with respect to gender problems do not lend themselves to predominantly quantitative measurement.

All of these factors have limited the impacts of positive changes. Yet the benefits of the groundswell created by the 1995 World Conference on Women, the most participatory United Nations event in history, which mobilized women at the grassroots level throughout the world, are still being realized. Many humanitarian personnel, consultants, constituents, and donors continue to push for gender-related programs. Positive change has also come about in response to increased reporting on abuses against women by human rights organizations, and by media coverage of wartime sexual violence. Moreover, international law, which is itself evolving, has provided a firm basis for recognizing women's rights as human rights and for stigmatizing wartime sexual violence as a violation of humanitarian law. Thus humanitarian action focusing on gender continues to come into sharper focus, however uneven and, at times, mistaken in approach.

With cautious optimism, this book explains this mixed progress of recent years. Chapter 1 provides analytical tools for approaching gender and suggests the ways in which women experience war differently from men. Chapter 2 reviews recent experience in three major crises: Bosnia, Kosovo, and Afghanistan. Chapter 3 outlines the supportive framework offered by international law. Conclusions and recommendations form the subject of Chapter 4. The study uses non-technical language in order to be accessible to a wide group of students, academics, policymakers, and humanitarian and human rights practitioners. It seeks to stimulate debate on the ways war affects women and how humanitarian organizations should respond. It finds that attempts by humanitarian groups to provide assistance and protection will fall short unless women are enlisted as major participants in the process.

# INTRODUCING A GENDER PERSPECTIVE IN HUMANITARIAN ACTION

## Introduction: Goals and Directions

CONVERGING LEGAL, POLITICAL, and social developments in the 1990s have focused unprecedented world attention on gender-based violence and gender bias in many conflicts. The UN, governments, and nongovernmental organizations (NGOs), however, have not responded to the needs of affected women. These needs include physical safety and freedom from violence; economic and educational opportunities; physical, psychological, and reproductive health care; and adequate food for themselves and their families.

The UN Commission on the Status of Women has pointed out that war-affected women face discrimination in access to relief supplies and are included in only token numbers in decision-making on humanitarian work.[1] "Women occupy a subordinate position in society," one recent study has observed, "which often makes them targets for physical attacks and abuse, blocks avenues for acquiring necessary skills, and limits their access to resources and power structures."[2] As a result, they face serious obstacles in bringing human rights and asylum claims successfully to international attention.

The UN High Commissioner for Refugees (UNHCR) has developed guidelines for considering the protection claims of women refugees, but field implementation has been uneven. Furthermore, although increased attention has been paid to the needs of internally displaced persons (IDPs), protection efforts are often still designed to reach only those who can fit the strict legal definition of refugee, leaving out the vast majority of women imperiled by conflict.[3]

This book analyzes the attempts of international and domestic actors to solve the human rights and humanitarian problems of women refugees, internally displaced women, and other women imperiled by war, with particular attention to innovative practices and to postwar reconstruction activities. The assistance and protection that humanitarian organizations seek to provide need to be understood as part of larger historical trends and legal and political developments. Evolving international human rights and humanitarian law provide a framework through which gender problems and inequities can be recognized and resolved.

An understanding of this framework can help humanitarian workers to be more sensitive to the gender-related aspects of assistance and protection and to be more effective in their mission. This book provides a holistic context for such work, informed by the historic treatment of gender-based violence and bias in wartime, by recent developments in human rights and humanitarian law and policy, and by the international recognition of violence against women as a human rights issue.

All of these elements, the analysis holds, are gendered: that is, they are influenced by real and perceived roles and needs of men and women in society.[4] The responses of humanitarian agencies to local customs and situations also are gendered: that is, they are influenced by differences between men's and women's roles in societies. This book examines wartime and postwar efforts to address gender-based violence and bias, highlighting both good practices and missed opportunities.

By use of the terms violence and bias, this book refers to discrimination and protection issues broadly. "Discrimination" refers to state-conducted or state-condoned abuse and deprivations of human rights based on gender, such as the specific targeting of women and girls for rape. Discrimination also refers to bias, lack of equal access, and obstacles to equal participation in assistance programs. "Protection" concerns the safeguarding of women from discrimination and other forms of abuse. Protection may be both physical and legal. Guarding women from attackers is an example of physical protection; giving asylum to women who face persecution is an instance of legal protection. Other protection actions include the need to protect women and girls from rape, forced prostitution, genital mutilation, torture, murder, and deprivation of human rights and needs such as food, clothing, shelter, water, and access to health care.[5]

The analysis identifies links between gender factors and humanitarian assistance and proposes directions for future change. It seeks to

- educate a wide audience regarding relevant historical, legal, and political developments about gender-based violence and bias in wartime and with regard to assistance and protection;

- improve understanding of the human rights issues facing refugee, displaced, and imperiled women, and of innovations designed to safeguard the rights of this population in complex emergencies;

- encourage policy changes to improve and apply international, regional, and national policies concerning gender problems in wartime;

- spur advocacy efforts by human rights groups employing a gender perspective to mainstream gender equality by "recognizing the different needs, interests and responsibilities of women and men and building more equitable gender relations";[6] and

- offer recommendations to improve the sensitivity to gender problems in humanitarian activities.

## Scope of Study

### Refugee, Displaced, and War-Imperiled Women

Today an estimated forty to fifty million people around the world are uprooted. Approximately 75 to 80 percent of them are women and children.[7] There are several reasons why women may be forced from their homes in wartime and peacetime.

*Internal and regional strife.* Women flee with their children when targeted by war and other forms of intra- and interstate violence and political unrest. Since civil war began in Somalia in 1991, for example, over a quarter of the population has fled. Three hundred thousand of these refugees sought safety in Kenya, where hundreds of women have been raped in camps in the northeastern provinces.[8] Throughout Peru's twelve-year internal war, women were the targets of sustained and frequently brutal violence, including rape and murder, to punish those believed to be sympathetic to the opposing side.[9] During the 1994 genocide, Rwandan women were subject to sexual violence on a massive scale.[10] As many as five thousand women in Rwanda were impregnated by rape, many of them by the killers of their spouses and family members.[11] In the 1980s thousands of Mozambican refugee women were raped after they sought shelter in Zimbabwe.[12]

*Human rights violations.* Women who experience abuse or are human rights activists face threats and violence that force them to flee to save their lives and protect their dignity and health. For example, in peace-time, women may attempt to leave their countries to escape battering in the home that is ignored by their governments or to avoid community practices dangerous to them such as female genital mutilation (FGM), the practice of child brides, forced sterilization, abortion, shock treat-ment, or other abuse of women in same-sex relationships. In wartime, women may flee in order to escape threats of sexual violence and other human rights abuses.[13] Human rights violations can cause flight in war-time and peacetime.

*Severe forms of bias and abuse based on alleged political activities.* Women may be pushed from their homes when government, military, paramilitary troops, or other powers severely discriminate against them and their families for political activities. Women human rights activists may flee so that their government does not harass their politically ac-tive family members, or women in flight may themselves face violence due to their relationship with political activists.[14] Some Albanian women in Kosovo, for example, have been forced to flee with their families after Serbian authorities accused them of supporting militant factions.[15]

*Severe forms of bias and abuse due to religion, race, ethnic group, or political opinion.* Women also leave their homes in order to escape health- and life-threatening forms of discrimination and persecution due to their religion, race, ethnic group, and political opinion. Examples include growing violence against Jews in the former Soviet Union, Roma or gypsies in Central and Eastern Europe, Muslims in Burma, and Chris-tians in the Sudan. Often gender-based abuse has at its core the failure of governments to respect different political or religious views.[16]

*Natural disasters and environmental degradation.* Women attempt to protect themselves and their families from natural disasters that force millions to move in search of shelter, safety, and work. Environmental causes of movement may include nuclear or chemical disasters, defores-tation, severe air pollution, global warming, and drought-induced famine.[17]

*Poor economic conditions.* Women now constitute the majority of mi-grant workers who must look for employment outside their country. In war-torn countries, women often find themselves unable to support them-selves and their families and thus are forced to seek employment across state borders. In newly deregulated economies of the former Soviet Union and Eastern Europe, many skilled women workers have been unable to find jobs providing a living wage and have faced state-condoned discrimination against working women.[18]

All of the above causes of flight collectively contribute to the largest population shifts ever encountered. Significantly, the types of protections afforded to uprooted people under international law depend largely upon their reason for flight. This book deals with uprooted women who fall within the three categories of refugees, internally displaced, or war-imperiled.

"Refugees" are people who are forced to leave their home country because of fear of persecution based on certain specific grounds examined below. "Displaced persons" are people who leave their homes to flee persecution but who stay within the borders of their home country. Worldwide, the proportion of internally displaced people has increased relative to the number of refugees.[19] "War-imperiled populations" is a non-technical term that includes all populations in conflict situations, including those who may not have left their homes.

Women and girls in all three categories face common problems such as discrimination and lack of legal autonomy and vulnerability to violence. However, their legal status differs in significant ways. International conventions protect refugees but not displaced persons or those otherwise imperiled by war. Moreover, in the case of IDPs, the very government that has caused their displacement often has the primary responsibility for their protection, thus complicating access and provision of protection and assistance.[20] As Roberta Cohen has observed, "Often they are caught up in internal conflicts between their governments and opposing forces. Some of the highest mortality rates ever recorded during humanitarian emergencies have come from situations involving internally displaced persons. There is . . . no one international organization with responsibility for providing protection and assistance to the internally displaced."[21]

Several cases of severe deprivation and abuse of internally displaced women have been documented by Judy Benjamin.[22] Burundi women refugees living in Tanzanian camps, for example, received far greater protection and assistance than displaced Rwandan women living in their own country. In the refugee camps in neighboring countries, provision was made for health care services, food rations, skill training, and the education of children. In addition, UNHCR protection officers monitored the grounds to ensure physical safety. In the camps for the internally displaced, by contrast, none of these services was available and women had no mechanisms for reporting sexual violence and other forms of exploitation.[23] "As traumatic to women as any displacement may be, usually the circumstances are worse for internally displaced persons than for refugees, even though their needs are similar."[24]

In recognition of the needs of populations who do not fit the legal definition of refugee, UNHCR increasingly includes internally displaced persons in its mandate. While this book refers explicitly to refugee women when discussing the legal definition of refugees and the grounds for recognition of gender-based persecution, the underlying concepts apply also to displaced and war-imperiled populations.

## Overview of Women in War

Civilians, especially women, children, the elderly, and the disabled, are often victims of bias and abuse in situations of conflict,[25] which range from armed international or civil wars to state-sponsored or state-condoned human rights violations against political, racial, ethnic, national, or religious minorities. As recognized by the Beijing Women's Conference, such abuse includes "torture and cruel, inhumane and degrading treatment or punishment, summary or arbitrary executions, disappearances, arbitrary detentions, all forms of racism and racial discrimination, foreign occupation and alien domination, xenophobia, poverty, hunger and other denials of economic, social and cultural rights, religious intolerance, terrorism, discrimination against women and lack of the rule of law."[26] Recent studies have helped dispel "the myth that women, like children, are incidental and not direct targets of persecution, or that their suffering, whether targeted or not, is insufficiently severe . . ."[27] Only after governments and nongovernmental organizations fully appreciate that attacks on women are part of war strategy can they take steps to address protection needs.

Government, paramilitary, and other opponents usually target women as a result of their ethnic, national, religious, racial, and/or political affiliations. But there is a gender component as well. They use gender as an effective tactic for attacking all of the group identities listed on the next page, as well as attacking women as women and men as men. The subservient position of women throughout much of the world fosters conditions in which women are subject to abuse and left without recourse to fight it and prevent future wrongs. "Adding to this disadvantaged state, refugee women find themselves outside of what familiar institutions do exist in their native States, and often unable to communicate in their new environments."[28] Unaccompanied women and girls are particularly vulnerable to protection infringement because they are removed from the community structures that could shield them

## Human Rights Abuses against Women

A pregnant woman detainee is punched in the stomach by police officers. An elderly woman is raped in front of her family by armed guards. A young girl is detained and sexually humiliated by government agents. A wife is tortured by interrogators to force her husband to "confess." A mother is shot dead by soldiers simply because her son is suspected of political activities. A daughter is threatened with death by government agents because she has asked after her "disappeared" father.

The list of such gross human rights violations against women is endless. Many are targeted because they are strong, because they are political activists, community organizers, or persistent in demanding that their rights or those of their relatives are respected. Others are targeted because they are seen as vulnerable, young women who can easily be sexually abused or humiliated, frightened mothers who will do anything to protect their children, pregnant women who fear for their unborn babies, women who can be used to get at men, or refugee women who are isolated and vulnerable in unfamiliar surroundings."

*Source*: Amnesty International, *Women on the Front Line* (New York: Amnesty International, 1991), 7.

from abuse.[29] In addition, the reproductive role of women makes many of them less mobile and more susceptible to physical abuse.[30]

Women in conflict often suffer abuses and consequences different from those visited upon men. Throughout history soldiers have raped women as a calculated part of war strategy.[31] Mass rapes of women have been documented in recent years in such diverse countries as Bosnia, Cambodia, Haiti, Peru, Somalia, and Uganda.[32] Ruth Seifert identifies the following characteristics of wartime rape: (1) rape has been treated as part of the "rules of war" as a right mainly conceded to victors; (2) in military conflicts the abuse of women is part of male communication, graphic demonstration of triumph over men who fail to protect "their" women; (3) wartime rape is also justified by acceptance of the notion that soldiers are "naturally" masculine and that masculinity is naturally violent; (4) rapes committed in war are aimed at destroying the adversary's culture; (5) orgies of rape originate in culturally ingrained hatred of women that is acted out in extreme situations.[38] Rape is an effective weapon of war.

Numerous studies show that rape is an extreme act of violence perpetrated by sexual means. Seifert explains that rape in war or peacetime is not primarily sexual but an act of aggression: "Rape is not an aggressive expression of sexuality, but a sexual expression of aggression. In the perpetrator's psyche, it does not fulfill sexual functions, but is a manifestation of anger, violence and domination of a woman. The purpose is to degrade, humiliate and subjugate her."[34]

While men sometimes also experience rape and sexual violence in wartime, women are targeted in particular, often as a way to humiliate and defeat the men in the community. As Susan Brownmiller has observed:

[Rape] by a conqueror is compelling evidence of the conquered's status of masculine impotence. Defense of women has long been a hallmark of masculine success. Rape by a conquering soldier destroys all remaining illusions of power and property for men of the defeated side. The body of a raped woman becomes a ceremonial battlefield, a parade ground for the victor's trooping of the colors. The act that is played out upon her is a message passed between men—vivid proof of victory for one and loss and defeat of the other.[35]

Women are targeted for sexual abuse as property of the enemy nation and as women.[36] In this sense, women are "doubly dehumanized—as woman, as enemy. . . . In one act of aggression, the collective spirit of women and of the nation is broken, leaving a reminder long after the troops depart."[37]

Fear of violence also has a particular impact upon women. Fear of rape and fear of being caught in the crossfire, for example, may cause women to stay at home or to hide. Fear of violence limits women's ability to go to work, gather fuel, shop, or stand in line for humanitarian aid. For women with children, fear of violence entails the constant stress of looking after their children's movements.

In military culture, sexual abuse of women has been described as "standard operating procedure."[38] Rape of enemy women is expected. In addition to acts of individual soldiers that are not necessarily planned though usually condoned, sexual violence may also be part of a strategy to terrorize a population. Furthermore, when women are tortured during interrogation or imprisonment in times of war and peace, the torture may be of a sexual nature. In times of conflict, women lose the traditional protections they might have from sexual abuse and are prey to

## Girl Soldiers

Underage girl soldiers appear in most of today's estimated thirty-two armed conflicts around the world. Camps for refugee and internally displaced persons are often prime recruiting grounds. Girl soldiers are often worse off than boys. In addition to performing military service, many are also forced to provide sexual services to combatants. Girl solders are known to be used for the most hazardous and inhumane military operations such as serving as suicide bombers and clearing mines.

All child soldiers face particular problems in demobilizing and reintegrating into their families and communities. Once a child has joined an armed group, he or she is regarded as having completely broken with a traditional role in society. For these children, there is no return. Researchers have found the problem particularly pronounced for girl children. This may at least partly account for phenomena such as young female suicide bombers who often surpass their male comrades in fanaticism and commitment to the cause. When girl soldiers do manage to demobilize, difficulties in gaining acceptance in their communities and a lack of reintegration assistance such as education and vocational skills means that they sometimes end up in criminality and prostitution.

*Source*: UNHCR, *Refugee Women and UNHCR: Implementing the Beijing Platform for Action* (Geneva: UNHCR, 1998), 35

abuse by enemy soldiers and by civilians.[39]

In addition to direct violence against themselves, women deal with the violence committed against their loved ones. When men are attacked or imprisoned, women are frequently left alone to take care of their families and to work for the release of male family members.[40] In war, male emasculation often leads to domestic violence. Domestic violence is defined as violence among members of a family or members of the same household. While any person in a household could be the target, domestic violence is most frequently experienced by women.[41]

Domestic violence involves physical and sexual violence as well as the breaching of reproductive rights. Domestic violence also includes psychological abuse, such as forced isolation, humiliation, denial of support, and threats. Survivors of domestic abuse often consider psychological abuse to be even more devastating than physical assault.[42] Surveys on violence against women, although important measures of reported abuse, tend to underestimate the number and level of domestic violence. In wartime, women may be particularly unwilling to report domestic violence because of additional social taboos, especially where the male perpetrator is a victim of ethnic violence.

Conflict places the integrity of the family at issue. Women may be forced into new economic roles in wartime, particularly when their men are killed or missing. Most women refugees are without male family support. In some cases, the extended family may be retained. If the family is intact and a man is present, women must often deal with changes in male and female roles. Often the man, who used to work outside the home, is left without work, while the woman continues to be productive, at times providing for all basic needs of the family. This is one important cause of domestic violence. Many times the burden on women increases as their elderly relatives become more dependent. If the men do not adjust their roles, there is a danger of women becoming more and more overworked.[43]

Governments and nongovernmental organizations rarely recognize that often women and girls fight in armed conflict, either as formal soldiers or as loose-knit defense and paramilitary units. Their experiences in conflict and in demilitarization are gendered. While some communities celebrate women warriors, others ignore them. Women warriors often have great difficulty readjusting to their role as family caretakers.

Many former women and child (male and female) combatants were subjected to sexual abuse, either by the enemy or by their own comrades. This fact is too shameful for their communities to acknowledge; if the sexual abuse is made public, the community may reject the women altogether. Very few humanitarian organizations offer psychosocial counseling and rehabilitation for female soldiers. Psychosocial support generally is lacking in wartime for everyone.

## Needs of Uprooted Women

In addition to seeking physical protection from violence, a woman imperiled by war seeks assistance in providing adequate food, shelter, health care, and a sense of security to her family. Women's needs include access to adequate gynecological health care, sanitary products, nutritional supplements, pre- and postnatal care, and culturally sensitive psychosocial counseling. All of these must be met in the context of day-to-day life. A day in the life of uprooted women is marked by the following concerns, each of which have a gender aspect.

*Lack of protection from violence and other forms of abuse and exploitation.* Uprooted women are particularly vulnerable to intimidation, sexual abuse, and other forms of physical exploitation. They are vulnerable at all stages: in flight, in their country of refuge, and upon return to their home country. Unaccompanied women and girls are particularly at risk for sexual assault, often from the forces which are supposed to protect them. Long-term inhabitants of refugee camps are often lured into prostitution rings or made to perform sexual acts in return for food or favors such as an asylum hearing. Human rights groups have documented cases of women refugees or migrants being raped or sexually assaulted by border guards or security forces.[44]

*Depression, despondency, and feelings of hopelessness.* Women who flee their homes do not usually expect to be gone for long. As the days and months drag on, many women become increasingly depressed, and few have social services or counseling to help them.[45]

*Ruptured human contact.* Uprooted women often lose contact with their communities and family members, particularly males. They may be unable to find or contact those closest to them. They may have menfolk who have "disappeared" while in combat or in flight. They may know where some of their friends and family members are but are unable to contact them.

*Hostility, violence, and discrimination in host country or host region.* This may take the form of racism, economic discrimination, sexual harassment, sexual violence, or other forms of abuse. It can limit refugees' abilities to move outside their temporary homes or to find work. Burmese refugees in Thailand, for example, are not allowed to send their children to school, and Thai homeowners are not willing to rent them rooms or houses.[46]

*Inability to find meaningful work.* Some countries do not allow refugees to work legally, and women often do not have legal papers. Other countries discourage employment or provide opportunities that do not fully use women's skills. As a result, refugee and displaced women often work in low-paid, exploitative jobs where employers take advantage of their illegal status. In Croatia, where 80 percent of the 380,000 refugees are women, they are not allowed to work, "thus confining refugee women to absolute dependency on inadequate humanitarian assistance."[47]

*Lack of access to basic items needed for daily life.* Women usually have the burden of feeding and clothing their families. Also, aid packages often do not provide for women's needs such as gynecological care, stockings, and cosmetics. Groups that work with refugee women argue that such items are not a luxury: if given the choice, women refugees may ask for them before other things.[48] Despite improvements with respect to the provision of gender-specific aid packages, the prevailing understanding of "humanitarian essentials" may still evidence an implicit gender bias.[49]

*Lack of access to health care and other services.* Access to reproductive health care and contraception is crucial to a woman's well-being. However, such services are scarce or nonexistent in most refugee camps. Members on a fact-finding mission to Sarajevo in October 1993 found that as "women of Sarajevo have been used to family planning programs and the Pill, but neither [were] available," a very high rate of abortions were being performed in unsafe conditions by unqualified practitioners.[50] World Health Organization (WHO) officials in Haiti successfully argued that family planning devices should be among the items exempted from imports prohibited under international economic sanctions.

*Difficulty in extracting legal and administrative remedies.* Access to legal remedies is influenced by gender-related factors. Women persecuted because of their gender may have difficulty proving refugee status. In addition, women who are victims of military attack may have a hard time proving they are victims of persecution rather than random violence. Since some asylum officers still see sexual violence as random offenses, a soldier's rape of a woman may be discounted even though rape in war is recognized as a violation of international humanitarian law. Asylum officers often discount women's experiences of conflict as being "not severe enough" to constitute persecution.

## Gender Dimensions of Human Rights Violations

The concerns of uprooted women can be summarized with reference to the United Nations Development Fund for Women's (UNIFEM) four key gender dimensions of human rights violations.[51] The first is that human rights violations take different forms for women and men. As detailed above, women are targeted for persecution in wartime in ways that men are not. A second dimension focuses on gender-related circumstances that make it likely that women will suffer more from a human rights violation than men will. Wartime reduces accountability for atrocities; women are particularly vulnerable. Traditional gender roles make women more susceptible to gender-based violence and less able to find a paying job. The third gender-related aspect of human rights is that the consequences of violations can be gender-specific. Rape of a woman, for example, can lead to pregnancy; the uprooting of elderly people can lead to greater burdens for the women of the community. The final dimension, also explored above, is that gender-related factors may influence access to remedies. Legal prohibitions and cultural mores, for example, may constrain a woman from reporting sexual violence or from receiving the assistance needed.

People's strengths and weaknesses in responding to conflict are influenced by whether they are male or female; based on their different roles in society, women often identify different priorities than men do. The United Nations High Commissioner for Refugees has recognized the necessity of emphasizing the needs of war-imperiled women, in particular because they are most commonly overlooked: "Until needs assessment and participation of all segments of a target group are integral to good [humanitarian protection and assistance] planning, attention must be consistently drawn to refugee women. This will ensure that they are included in mainstream activities, not made peripheral to them or segregated into women's projects."[52]

Meeting the needs of women means more than designing programs that focus on women. Rather, humanitarian organizations should integrate the resources and needs of uprooted women in all aspects of their work. Good planning will not overlook the particular needs and skills women bring to their own displacement, flight, resettlement, and other problems. Good programs will maintain a strong focus on the role of local women who are most able to determine the needs of the affected population.

## Analytical Tools

The present study uses the gender approach that has emerged within the United Nations system. This approach, which involves an examination of the needs and roles of women and men in society, is useful for analyzing assistance and protection efforts in terms of equity

## Successful Protective Action in Kenya

In 1993 a project called Women's Victims of Violence Project was launched in the Dadaab camps in Kenya, where Somali refugees were persistently subjected to sexual violence. Live thorn bushes were planted around the sites to protect the women. UNHCR built houses for local police, trained them in the rights of refugee women to protection, and convinced them to station themselves within the camps. UNHCR engaged Kenyan women lawyers to train the police. The training included prosecution of rape cases, significantly reducing incidents of rape.

Despite all of these initiatives, attacks still occurred when women and girls left the camps to collect firewood. Most of the victims were Somali women who had been asked about their clan affiliation by Somali-speaking aggressors. This indicated that the attackers were probably within the Somali community itself. UNHCR staff worked with respected community members to initiate a campaign that sensitized men and women in the camp about violence against refugee women.

In 1996, anti-rape committees were established within the camps. The committee members, male and female elders from various clans, committed themselves to reducing the number of rapes and helping victims. Religious leaders spoke out against harboring rapists and encouraged people to support the victims. Thus far, the committees have been largely successful in convincing the community that rape is a crime, and that the women survivors are not to blame. Further, the capacity of the community to solve serious problems has been reestablished.

Source: UNHCR, *Refugee Women and UNHCR: Implementing the Beijing Platform for Action* (Geneva: UNHCR, 1998), 12.

and efficiency. Key concepts involved in this approach, drawing heavily on definitions in published works, include the following:

- *Gender*: "As sex refers to biologically determined differences between men and women, so gender refers to the social differences between men and women that are learned, changeable over time and have wide variations both within and between cultures."[53] "Gender refers to what it means to be a boy or girl, woman or man, in a particular society. It includes accepting such factors as age, class and ethnicity as variables to this."[54]

- *Gender Perspective*: This is the notion that problems and solutions should be examined with gender in mind. The concept of "gender perspectives . . . is based on an understanding that in all situations some perspective of interpreting reality is present. Historically, that perspective has most often been biased towards the male view. Accordingly, most perspectives in reality have not taken women's views and experiences into account, rendering the everyday violations of women's human rights invisible."[55] A gender perspective "recognizes, understands and utilizes the knowledge of gender differences in planning, implementing and evaluating programs and working relationships . . ."[56] The words gendered (as in humanitarian assistance is "gendered") and gendering (as in a "gendering" of assistance solutions) incorporate this notion of gender perspectives. These forms of the word gender emphasize when and how a gender lens may assist in solving a problem.

- *Gender-Specific Claims*: Human rights claims relating to the abuse women and men suffer because of their gender. For example, this refers to instances when human rights are being violated due at least partly to a person's gender and/or when women's experience of a human rights violation differs from men's experience due to gender-specific consequences or experiences.[57]

- *Gender Analysis*: Gender analysis examining both men and women and the social, economic, and cultural forces which shape their respective position.[58] As such, gender can be "a socioeconomic variable in the analysis of roles, responsibilities, constraints, opportunities and needs of men and women in any context. The use of the term 'gender' as an analytical tool focuses not on women as an isolated group, but on the roles and needs of men and women."[59] "Given that women are usually in a disadvantaged position as compared to men of the same socioeconomic level," gender analysis "usually means giving explicit attention to women's needs, interests and perspectives. The ultimate objective is the advancement of women's status in society."[60]

- *Gender-Based Violence*: Violence committed against women as women and against men as men—in other words, violence striking at what it means to be a man or a woman in a particular society. This includes violence particular to women, such as rape, sexual assault, female genital mutilation, or dowry burning, as well as violence against women for failing to conform to restrictive social norms.[61] Sexual violence designed to emasculate men (such as mutilation of the male sex organs) is also gendered.

- *Violence Against Women*: Any act of gender-based violence that results in, or is likely to result in, physical, sexual, or psychological harm or suffering to women, including threats of such acts, coercion, or arbitrary deprivation of liberty, whether occurring in public or private life. Violence against women includes, but is not limited to: a) Physical, sexual, and psychological violence in the family, including battering, sexual abuse of female children in the household, dowry-related violence, marital rape, female genital mutilation and other traditional practices harmful to women, and non-spousal violence related to exploitation; b) Physical, sexual, and psychological violence occurring within the general community, including rape, sexual abuse, sexual harassment and intimidation at work, in educational institutions and elsewhere, and trafficking in women and forced prostitution; c) Physical, sexual, and psychological violence perpetrated or condoned by the state, wherever it occurs.[62]

- *Women's Human Rights*: Women's rights are human rights, that is, rights to which women are entitled simply by being human. A political strategy informed by this principle introduces a focus on women into the human rights movement and, conversely, an emphasis on human rights principles into the women's rights movement. Like other human rights, women's human rights are related to one's dignity; they are universal, inalienable, indivisible, interconnected, and interdependent; governments are obligated to enforce such rights in a way that promotes equality and nondiscrimination.[63]

## Conclusion

This study examines how the intersection of human rights and humanitarian concerns is gendered. That is, each aspect of the existence of an uprooted and imperiled population can be seen through a gender lens. This is true with reference to the initial human rights violations, the type of violence and violations encountered during flight and in temporary encampments, and the consideration of permanent solutions for resettlement or return. At the same time, the mechanisms to deliver aid and the protection and resettlement or return of uprooted and imperiled people are gender-biased when their design is based on the model of a male fleeing civil persecution. The reality of female populations at risk challenges the traditional model, demanding new thinking and approaches.

This book highlights recent innovations as well as the need for new approaches. This chapter has focused generally on the issue of violence and has set forth the general thesis and terms for discussion. The next chapter deals with issues particular to women in situations of armed conflict in Bosnia-Herzegovina, Kosovo, and Afghanistan. These three case studies pertain to specific programmatic trends related to gender and human rights, noting both opportunities seized and missed.

# APPLYING A GENDER PERSPECTIVE

THIS CHAPTER APPLIES a gender analysis to humanitarian activities in three places: Bosnia-Herzegovina, Kosovo, and Afghanistan. These case studies draw extensively on first-hand fieldwork, including interviews with aid workers in the areas. While the case studies do not encompass conflicts in all regions around the world, they raise many of the problems that contemporary humanitarian actors encounter wherever they find themselves.

The three areas are significant in many respects. In all, Islam is a factor in the political and social situation and (rightly or wrongly) in aid considerations, particularly regarding gender assistance. At the same time, Islam plays a considerably different role in all three areas. Afghanistan is closely identified with Islam; the practice of the faith, which has changed over time, significantly affects the treatment of gender issues. In contrast, most Bosnian Muslims and Kosovar Albanians identify more with their European than their Islamic roots. In the former Yugoslavia, the term "Muslim" does not refer to people who practice the Muslim faith but to Slavs who converted to Islam during the Ottoman period. While most Kosovar Albanians are of the Islamic faith, they identify themselves as Albanian rather than as Muslims. Although the cultural practices of Bosnian Muslims and Kosovar Albanians affect gender issues, Islam itself is of lesser importance.

The conflicts in Bosnia and Kosovo also differ from Afghanistan and from most other conflicts in that they are both European and very high profile. Both factors are very important in light of today's donor practices and the central role of the media in drawing attention to or ignoring a conflict. Media attention and donor-driven assistance affect how governments and nongovernmental organizations approach gender needs in conflict-related assistance. As explained in this chapter, donor largesse both hinders and helps the country as well as those marginalized by lack of media or donor attention.

Kosovo and Bosnia also share a historical, temporal, and political context that differs from Afghanistan in several important ways and substantially affects assistance related to gender. The conflict in Afghanistan was a long-term, Cold War struggle that has become a protracted civil war since the Soviet pullout more than a decade ago. The evolution of that conflict sets the stage for what is happening in Afghanistan today, how women are affected, and how donors respond. The conflicts in Bosnia and Kosovo, in contrast, were short-term, post–Cold War, and more internal in nature.

In addition, the Kosovo case highlights the convergence of issues of national sovereignty and human rights. Since Kosovo is still part of a sovereign nation, the crisis in Kosovo forces governments and nongovernmental organizations to cope with the tension between human rights and sovereignty. Assistance and protection efforts play a role by defining the limits of sovereignty in the face of gross and systemic human rights violations. From this perspective as well, gender issues that raise human rights concerns are of critical importance.

The case of Bosnia was a turning point in international recognition of protection for women in conflict and in attempts by governments and aid workers to solve the problems of women and girls. Coming a few short years later, the Kosovo crisis provided an opportunity to assess whether lessons were learned from the Bosnia experience regarding gender assistance and, in particular, whether women were being included in decision-making positions in assistance efforts. Given the vast amount of aid resources devoted to the Balkans (as compared to crises in Africa, for example), the two case studies, taken together, illustrate what is done to solve gender problems when relatively ample resources are present. The case of Afghanistan illuminates another set of dilemmas often faced by aid workers: that is, how to work effectively within the boundaries set by political authorities while not perpetuating the abuses inherent in their rules.

Each case study begins with an overview of the problem and the background to the conflict. It then discusses assistance efforts generally and draws out specific programmatic trends related to gender. Finally it analyzes the gender impact of the assistance and protection efforts and notes some successes and lessons learned.

# Bosnia-Herzegovina: Uprooted Women

## Overview of the Problem

Bosnia illustrates that the nature of conflict has changed, both in the range of actors and the methods of violence. Increasingly, eruptions of violence are more likely to be internal than interstate, involving competing power struggles defined by ethnic, tribal, or national loyalties.[1] The main perpetrators in such struggles are often intrastate or transstate, such as paramilitary troops and/or leaders of competing nations or tribes. Civilians—women, children, and elderly men—are often the targets in these conflicts. One tactic is the wholesale forcible removal or killing of an entire segment of the population such as those deemed to belong to the enemy nation, tribe, or ethnic group. Hence the use of the term "ethnic cleansing." Extensive international media coverage of Bosnia brought into the world's living rooms images of intragroup conflict and wide-scale human rights abuses against civilian populations. Rape and sexual abuse of "enemy" women accompanied the policies of "ethnic cleansing" as part of a planned tactic of terror and abuse.[2]

In response to these changes in the nature of modern armed conflict and to the practice of "ethnic cleansing" in particular, innovations in protection have been devised to meet the needs of imperiled populations. These new approaches, including the creation of humanitarian corridors, safe areas, temporary protection, and open cities in which protection was guaranteed to returning minority populations, are described in great detail in a related study.[3] While such mechanisms have indeed represented significant developments in the approach to assistance and protection, they have fallen well short of expectations. In some instances, they created problems for protection in general and the needs of refugee and internally displaced women in particular. Certainly, gender-based violence has not disappeared. Moreover, assistance offered along with temporary protection measures often has not included adequate psychosocial services for survivors of gender-based violence or other kinds of abuse.

The reports of sexual violence from Yugoslavia galvanized international recognition of gender-based violence as a human rights issue and lent new impetus to analysis of the gendered nature of conflict and of humanitarian responses. With Bosnia as a backdrop to their demands, women's human rights advocates at the 1993 World Conference on Human Rights in Vienna extracted from individual states and international bodies a commitment to devote more attention to the needs and rights of women. The events in Bosnia prompted the transformation of United Nations High Commissioner for Refugees (UNHCR) Executive Committee statements on women into a set of comprehensive guidelines (as discussed in the following chapter). These events also led many aid organizations to undertake new programs to help women war victims with their legal and physical protection and psychosocial needs.

Throughout the war, women reported tremendous difficulty in obtaining legal documentation of their status for themselves and their children, especially if they had spouses or other family members who were fighting or imprisoned elsewhere. Local authorities were often suspicious if the woman or her husband were actual or perceived members of the enemy group, however defined. Some women from ethnically mixed marriages in Bosnia fled to Serbia at the beginning of the war in 1992 to protect their children. Many of these women opposed the policies of Serbian nationalist forces in Bosnia and elsewhere in Yugoslavia, but they had no place to flee except to relatives in Serbia. Serbian authorities and local Serbs working with international aid organizations viewed these women as "belonging to their husbands" in Bosnia and thus refused to consider their requests for protection and assistance independently. If their husbands were not ethnically Serb, the women were especially mistrusted and denied benefits. If their husbands were Serb, the women were still assumed to be willing to return to Serbian-controlled parts of Bosnia.

The United Nations, the Organization on Security and Cooperation in Europe (OSCE), the European Community (EC), and other international, regional, and individual institutions adopted successive resolutions and declarations condemning war crimes and crimes against humanity in Bosnia, with special attention to sexual violence and abuse of women and girls. The media played a central role in exposing the problem and generating widespread public outrage against the violations. Still, diplomats dithered over a political solution and international military forces refused to take meaningful action to stop the violence and punish the aggressors. The only groups that responded at an early stage of the crisis were aid organizations, many funded by state donors that used assistance as a way to conceal their failure to halt the bloodshed and to placate those who demanded a more direct response.

The first war in recent years that a European could hitchhike to observe,[4] Bosnia became the favorite focus of Western assistance groups and journalists. They arrived in droves, with most aid operations commencing in 1993 and escalating with the signing of the Dayton Peace Accord in 1995. The number of international NGOs with offices in

## Refugees from Bosnia: One Story

### Woman, 38 years old, from Teslic

"We stayed for two years from the beginning of the war. We lived in fear but nobody touched us at first. I was alone in the house. My husband is an Albanian who works in Macedonia. We were afraid that if some people got killed, [the neighbors] would no longer say hello to us, as if we were the ones who did it. It was our neighbors, not the refugees who came into our village. I won't blame the ones who are not guilty.

"I came to this Hungarian camp a year ago, not knowing what would happen next. I came with my children of nineteen and seven years old. I took only a few things with me. We had to have one thousand German marks per person and another five hundred marks to pay the municipal authorities. You have to have a thousand papers to get out.

"My cousin was killed in his house, that is why we left. A neighbor killed him in the middle of the night, because his brother was killed on the front line. Even though my cousin was a Muslim volunteering in the Serbian army, wounded when fighting for his village. . . . The police came and they took the murderer to prison in Banja Luka, but what is the use of it? Three days later, young men between the ages of twenty-five and thirty massacred a man in our village only because his name was Alija.

"Before the war we didn't know who was what, we all had our houses next to each other: in my village Serbs and Muslims lived together. My best friend was a Serbian woman, but they cannot protect us now, because now they call us *balije* [a derogatory name for Muslim]. I don't even know what it means.

". . . They harassed me and another woman in the village. I worked in a neighbor's house and I would stay there to sleep because I was afraid to be alone in my house with the children. I went at dusk to my place with my son just to feed our cow. A man came up to my front door with a mask over his face. He took me by my hand and dragged me outside the house. My son saw it. This man dragged me to the stable. I fought back but he stripped off my clothes. He took me to the back of the house and started to kiss me, saying "You are a woman, you must give yourself to me." . . . When I took the mask off his face and recognized him as a neighbor I felt even worse, I got more afraid. So often he had sat at our place, drank coffee with us. . . .

"He raped me. I told nobody because I didn't want to cause panic. Not even my husband. I am afraid of blood revenge. That must not happen. My son saw it, but even he keeps quiet.

"This man wanted to come every day and rape me, and he was young enough to be my son; he also was only nineteen. That is why I left, I couldn't defend myself. He could do anything he wanted. We had no rights. Once in the post office they didn't even let me send a letter to my husband . . . The same in the shops; they had known me for years and suddenly they didn't speak to me, they just wanted me out of the way."

*Source*: Julie Mertus, ed. et al., *The Suitcase: Refugee Voices from Bosnia and Croatia* (Berkeley: University of California Press, 1997), 28–30. Used with permission.

Bosnia then tapered off in 1998 when donors began to lose interest and to focus attention elsewhere. As of early 1999, an estimated 170 to 240 international NGOs maintained offices in Bosnia[5] and tens of thousands of foreigners calling themselves aid workers lived there. Dominated by North Americans and western Europeans, the international aid community also included a large number of nongovernmental and governmental organizations from the Middle East (Iran, Kuwait, Saudi Arabia, United Arab Emirates) and Japan.

In many respects, Bosnia presents an ultimate test case for the limitations of the efforts by aid groups struggling with gender problems. Compared with other crises, a tremendous amount of funding and resources was potentially available for work on gender issues. Given the scale of resources received, the largest NGOs at work in Bosnia can no longer be considered fully nongovernmental; growth in funding sources from governments means more governmental influence in NGO operations. A number of the NGOs at work in Bosnia claim to be responsive to women affected by war. The problem in Bosnia is not the absence of donor largesse. Instead, the massive scale of funding and the perceived need to be "doing something" reinforced the prevailing insensitivity toward gender problems and lack of listening to community-based groups. Funding also affects the potential leverage and effectiveness of such organizations. The role and relevance of indigenous organizations and their ability to act independently of outside influences are crucial in finding ways to solve gender problems effectively in armed conflict and its aftermath.

## Assistance and Protection Efforts

The first assistance programs introduced in Bosnia were emergency relief programs, aimed at providing food, water, basic health care, materials for shelter, and other relief to populations in crisis.[6] These programs began at the onset of the conflict in 1992 and continued to occupy aid workers until the signing of the Dayton Peace Accord in 1995. Mechanisms for aid distribution were altered to adjust to the nature of warfare in Bosnia, where political and military leaders targeted civilians for particular abuse. The goal of military campaigns was not to win battles against opposing troops, as in conventional warfare, but to terrorize, push out, and otherwise eliminate "enemy" groups from desired areas, replacing them with one's own group. Convoys channeled aid to pockets of civilians living in areas under siege, to uprooted persons in flight, and to those who had settled in private accommodations, camps, and other temporary facilities.

The distinction between refugee, displaced, and war-imperiled populations became blurred early on in Bosnia. Organizations established to aid "refugees" such as UNHCR and its implementing partners expanded their mandates to provide assistance to all in need, without reference to their legal status under traditional international refugee law (see Chapter 3). This approach helped women and children because they were less likely to be able to prove refugee status and more likely to be considered internally displaced.

Under such conditions, humanitarian groups found themselves confronted with a number of protection problems. Some were directly related to delivering emergency assistance. When the goal was to force civilians to abandon their homes, particularly in 1993 to 1995, warring factions were not willing to allow the type of access by humanitarian organizations that would have permitted civilians to stay in their home towns—at least not unless the aid brought some other benefits such as assistance for their own soldiers or "their own" civilians. Humanitarian organizations that refused or failed to broker deals became targets of warring factions.

# Bosnia-Herzegovina and the Federal Republic of Yugoslavia

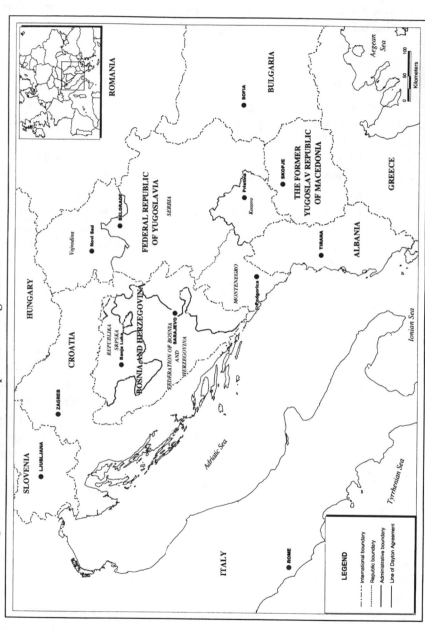

LEGEND

- - - - - International boundary
.......... Republic boundary
_____ Administrative boundary
_____ Line of Dayton Agreement

Extraordinary efforts such as airdrops and military-escorted convoys were used throughout the war in Bosnia to deliver aid to civilians living in cities under siege. Since most of the young men in these areas were fighting on a full- or part-time basis in the military, the bulk of the aid went to women, children, and older men. The recipients, while grateful, complained about much of the aid failing to help them. For example, they received outdated foods and medicines, oversupplies of some foodstuffs, and a complete lack of others such as nutrients for nursing mothers. A culture that did not use tampons was sent a vast supply.[7]

As populations moved across boundaries and borders, with a large wave in 1993 to 1994, aid workers assumed some responsibility for legal protection, at times documenting flight and providing assessments for refugee status. Confronted with people who had suffered tremendous human rights violations and/or who faced the threat of such violations, aid workers found themselves asked to cooperate with legal documentation of such abuses and, in some cases, to offer physical protection for endangered refugees.

Many aid groups refused to work openly on protection concerns beyond documentation for fear of jeopardizing their principle of neutrality. In their view, protection work would entail taking sides among the various combatants. Some workers quietly cooperated with organizations conducting human rights documentation.

A few humanitarian organizations went further and reassessed their policies to increase their ability to provide protection. The kinds of physical protection humanitarian organizations could provide ranged from ad hoc decisions to physically safeguard a certain refugee population to the deliberate placement of an aid office to lend protection to the nearby population.[8] Aid delivery itself became a means of protection, with food and shelter offering a form of protection from human rights abuses. Some aid workers even trucked out war-affected populations from areas in conflict and hid endangered people when the need arose.

The linkages between assistance, protection, and human rights was of particular concern to the many women in Bosnia who experienced rape or other gender abuse or faced the threat of these and other human rights violations. Fear of gender violence was one of the reasons women cited in leaving their homelands; in addition, they faced the threat of gender violence in flight and at their place of temporary shelter. Many sought assistance in leaving the place in which they were abused and in obtaining legal and physical protection. Some of them were willing to tell humanitarian and human rights workers about their own personal abuse but many more would not, especially if they were raped or otherwise sexually violated and if the person to whom they were to account their story was foreign and/or male.

Journalists flocked to Bosnia, asking to interview "raped women," and some foreign humanitarian groups set up offices and treatment facilities for "raped women."[9] Women refused to identify themselves by that single criterion. Doing so would open themselves up to criticism and shame within their own communities, affecting prospects for future marriage and family life. So instead many women preferred to remain silent, complicating the efforts of protection officers to document persecution.

Some of the earliest attempts of international donors to aid women who had been raped in Bosnia and in Croatia involved misguided attempts to establish facilities specifically for "raped women." Most women would not go near such a project for fear of identifying themselves to their communities. Survivors of sexual abuse received meaningful health care and counseling through broader projects established to aid all women or all members of a community. Within the context of a safer program that did not require women to identify themselves as sexually abused, some did tell about their experiences. Even without doing so, all women received assistance.

The measures by which local and international humanitarian groups awarded assistance failed to account for gender violence and abuse. Some, such as the International Organization for Migration (IOM), gave priority in relocation programs to survivors of concentration camps and/or torture. But raped women were largely excluded because they were not considered to be parts of those populations. Most of these survivors were male and thus a disproportionate percentage of male applicants to IOM were moved while a disproportionate number of females were denied.[10] Women had little chance of being moved unless they were attached to a man who had survived; women whose husbands were missing or fighting back home had little chance of having a successful independent assessment of their claim.

Rape and other violence against women were viewed as a side effect of war and not as a part of military strategy. This situation changed slightly in 1994 when IOM modified its policies to permit women who were sexually assaulted to receive priority, but even then IOM officers spoke of doubts about credibility and suspected many of the women of lying.[11]

The UNHCR Guidelines on the Protection of Refugee Women and UNHCR guidelines on sexual violence did not exist at the onset of the war. Even after guidelines were promulgated, many aid workers did not know of their existence or, if they did, failed to follow them. "We did not have time," "They were not really relevant," "There are just too many guidelines," they would complain. Yet, public pressure ensured that humanitarian organizations faced up to wartime gender violence and, although far from perfect, major strides were taken to adjust programming to help war-affected women in Bosnia.

*Innovative Responses.* Bosnia illustrates well the trend in aid to move from emergency assistance to developmental relief, or assistance as part of a longer term project of reconstruction and redevelopment.[12] Aid agencies have long worked in all sectors of society, including health, democratization, reconstruction, food aid, community development, repatriation, NGO capacity building, psychosocial work, agriculture, shelter, and income generation.

The first large wave of such developmental relief projects focusing on gender problems in Bosnia was established to give counseling and other support to survivors of rape. Some of the psychosocial programs were implemented with the help of locally trained health care professionals; many of these projects were well-received as culturally appropriate and extremely necessary. However, efforts that got underway as early as the end of 1992 and early 1993 also often involved well-intentioned but ill-conceived plans using outsiders for mental health counseling and statistics gathering. Many projects would send in an ill-prepared outside expert to give workshops to local health care providers, many of whom were by that time far more experienced than the outsider in dealing with wartime trauma. While some of these flawed projects were closed down, many remain in place today. In fact, in order to receive funding from donor agencies for their own projects, local health care workers must still suffer through culturally inappropriate training.

Parallel to the funding of mental health projects for women was the effort of international aid organizations to build local female NGOs to work on women's concerns. One of the largest and earliest efforts to build the capacity of local women is Delphi International's Star Project, which supports non-nationalistic and multiethnic women's organizations throughout the former Yugoslavia with networking, training, and project support. More recent approaches include a lightly funded but high-impact program of the OSCE Democratization Project that brings individual women and female employees of NGOs from all parts of Bosnia together to increase the involvement of women in politics.[13]

By bringing women from different geographic regions and national backgrounds together, the OSCE and Star Project support practical work on conflict resolution. Discussions are framed not in terms of ethnonational tensions but of some specific subject matter, such as women in politics generally. Intergroup understanding is built as diverse groups work together to solve common problems. The difficulty with such an approach is that some of the gatherings failed to result in any concrete actions. Even though the Star Project has experienced some success at encouraging communication across ethnic lines, most local women's NGOs in many parts of Bosnia continue to be composed predominately of one ethnic group.

Some of the local women's NGOs developed gradually, from kitchen-table endeavors to full office enterprises. Others were created by internationals, handpicked by foreigners to implement a preconceived notion of humanitarian work for women. While the former Yugoslavia had a handful of academically oriented feminist organizations and pro forma state-mandated women's groups, most women who found themselves working for women's groups during the war had never previously worked on gender problems. International groups created many of the programs in their own image, at times sensitive to cultural differences and at times blatantly insensitive to local variations. This crippled the ability of indigenous NGOs to work effectively.

Local women became savvy about the aid process and tried their best to derive some benefit from the assistance that came their way. Nonetheless, extensive bureaucracy, paperwork, and short time frames for project completion clashed with local desires for flexibility and longer term community growth. In return for working for such an endeavor, local people often received high salaries and the ability to squeeze in their own ideas for improving the status of women. "We took the money and went to the training and then did what we had to do," one local staffer said.[14] This often meant that the local people implemented projects in line with their own desires and not with particular attention to donor concerns, although they genuinely believed that they were abiding by the agreed-upon plan.

Gender issues within international humanitarian organizations working in Bosnia have favored the employment of local women. Expatriate and local women have long worked for international aid organizations in Bosnia, albeit not on parity with men in management positions. Given that local men were more likely to be fighting or imprisoned than local women, the majority of local people employed as translators and staff have generally been women. Young, educated, urban women had the best chances of being hired because they were most likely to speak English or other foreign languages. To the extent that a foreign NGO could find a local NGO partner, for the same reasons the local partner was most likely to be predominately composed of women.

Some of the local women's NGOs were formed spontaneously to deal with local problems and to take advantage of the international funding available to women's groups. Others came about as a result of conversion of projects established by international agencies "wanting to leave something behind," or by local staff "wanting to strike out on their own."[15] Viva Zena in Tuzla was originally a project funded by a group of individual German donors to support women and orphans. Three different organizations named "Amica" are in the process of establishing themselves as inheritors of projects established by a small German organization, Amica.[16]

Bospo and Bosfam in Tuzla were the beneficiaries of activities initiated by the Danish Refugee Council and Oxfam, respectively. A highly successful women-run microcredit project of the International Rescue Committee in Tuzla is in the process of becoming fully independent.[17] Similarly, Medica was originally a German group and the Bosnia branches were German-initiated. Now independent, Medica Zenica (its current name) offers an array of services, including psychosocial support, an *infoteka* serving as a library, research, and information source, a clearing house on domestic violence, and a legal support group.[18]

Experience such as this suggests that the creation of self-sustaining local women's NGOs is the exception and not the rule. Nearly every women's NGO in Bosnia today relies on international sources for support, many on a single donor. For example, Zene za Zene u Bosni (Women for Women in Bosnia) was set up entirely by foreign women and it remains dependent wholly on foreign sources for support.[19] This group, like many NGOs, faces the risk of being cut off by its funders at any moment. The popularity of capacity-building projects for NGOs appears to be a matter of rhetoric rather than a serious objective. Many women's NGOs have been abruptly and unceremoniously dumped by their original funder after the internationals completed their own missions, exhausted their funds, or simply became distracted by crises elsewhere.

In general, women's aid groups in Bosnia suffer from the same major problem as other groups there: the unusual position of NGOs in Bosnian society. To some extent, it can be said that the nongovernmental sector is the only sector that functions. NGOs assume the role of government, which does not provide social services, and the commercial and private sector, which is also quiescent. As a result, internationals have stepped in to fund local NGOs without sustainability or realism. Small NGOs, and in particular small European NGOs, were instrumental in the creation of many local NGOs in Bosnia, funded them for a while, and then dropped them when funds ran out. This killed enthusiasm among local NGOs and generated powerful competition for funding from outside groups.[20]

Many local organizations were at one time a source of cheap service delivery for foreign donors. When their usefulness ended, so did the foreign support. Several of the largest aid organizations operating in Bosnia also used local counterparts as cheap labor. So, too, did the tiny NGOs that hunted around Bosnia for women's groups to embrace their particular agenda. Most internationals had good intentions of fostering the local NGO sector by channeling funding and work through them. Yet nearly all of them created dependency. Local organizations were forced to adapt to the ever-changing demands of internationals or cease to exist. International groups should listen to indigenous groups and act accordingly. Instead, the process has run the other way around with indigenous groups continually doing the responding.

More recently, donors have shifted their priorities from emergency assistance and psychosocial work to reconstruction, microenterprise development, and income generation. The current catchwords are "reconstruction and reconciliation."[21] Psychosocial work and health projects have been jettisoned, leaving NGOs that work on such projects in "despair for the people with whom they work."[22] Projects for and by women have not escaped. To survive in Bosnia, NGOs have had to jump on the women's microenterprise and income generation bandwagon. For some groups this merely requires reframing existing projects. For example, the Mostar-based women's group, Zene BiHi, used to offer knitting and handicraft projects for women that were framed as "therapeutic work." Now the same projects are simply "work projects."[23]

Some microenterprise projects do succeed, for example, a sugar cube factory in Babunovici[24] and a greenhouse in Tuzla, but many of them fail. The problem with the many handicraft projects and similar endeavors is that they are not intended to produce competitive products in a market economy, either because it costs too much to make the goods or the goods simply are not attractive to market demand for fashionable products. "Those knitted slippers may sell to visiting American women, but who would buy them here?" one Bosnian woman activist wondered. "We need support for making real things that real women can wear."[25] Projects that once succeeded as therapy are now failing as enterprises.

Microenterprise and income-generating projects are also failing because many NGOs have a social welfare or emergency relief orientation and their staff is unequipped for economic development. Extensive training on microdevelopment cannot automatically turn off an aid worker's habitual assumptions and ways of operating. Called on now to establish projects that produce profitable products, some NGO staff refuse to embrace the new demands. As a result, microenterprise and income-generation projects have been set up with the knowledge that they will not in fact produce marketable goods and become self-sustaining.

Many of these projects are flawed from the start because they are designed and funded by an outside donor according to a preconceived formula without regard to realities on the ground. In one early effort adapting an approach that had proved successful elsewhere, pregnant cows were given to some of the most desperate women. The notion was that the women would be able to keep the calf after birth and kill the cow for meat. The problem was that the people were so desperate for food that they all killed the cows for meat while they were still pregnant.

Most microcredit programs for women in Bosnia fall within the "give a cow" genre in that they involve rural women while ignoring the huge number of trained professional women in urban areas. Some people contend that this approach is only natural since rural women represent the population in greatest need. This reasoning makes sense if microcredit and income-generating projects are considered relief projects, but not if they are envisioned as economic development undertakings. To the extent that microcredit and income-generating projects in Bosnia are designed to foster economic growth, they are flawed because they are not linked into larger economic reconstruction. Social services in Bosnia will continue to need outside support from international organizations or local government services.

The main postwar microcredit and income-generating funder,[26] the Bosnian Women's Initiative (BWI) was established by the United Nations in 1996 and funded with a $5 million contribution from the U.S. government and $155,000 from the Danish government. Since that time it has received an additional $1 million from the United States and support from the Japanese government, the Japanese Committee for Refugee Relief, and from the European Community Humanitarian Office (ECHO). (The U.S. contribution and the total pale in comparison with the over $45 million that the United States Agency for International Development (USAID) has spent on small business development projects in Bosnia that do not include enterprises headed by women.[27]) BWI funds primarily income-generating projects but also community service projects (support to NGOs, clubs, media), vocational training projects, microcredits, and psychosocial support. Sample projects included funding of a pig farm, bakery, greenhouse, tailoring workshop, beekeeping, strawberry and flower production, cheese production, graphic design workshop, and a computer graphic center. In line with general trends, psychosocial support in 1997 received only 2 percent of the BWI funding.[28]

Local women's groups criticize BWI for not working directly with them but instead channeling funds through "umbrella agencies" established in geographic regions of Bosnia. The decision-making process of the umbrella agencies is far from transparent; application procedures are cumbersome; and approval mechanisms are slow. In addition, a significant amount of funding is spent on foreign consultants and training instead of on direct programmatic work.[29] Since the appointment of a new BWI director, criticism has lessened somewhat. However, many formerly successful local women's groups remain unhappy with BWI's scope of operations.[30]

Other problems associated with the microcredit and income-generating orientation of many projects include the absence of a legal structure. This calls into question their legality and also their viability. BWI claims that "building the sustainability and capacity of local NGOs and women's associations is a high priority," but in fact BWI is not designed to provide the kind of follow-up support needed for sustainability. Projects most often must look elsewhere for that.[31] In addition, many of the local groups receiving microcredit financing have been funded far in excess of their capacity for good management. "There are organizations less than a year old charged with managing a project portfolio in excess of a million dollars, a supply-driven situation that represents little more than opportunism on the part of both donor and recipient."[32] Gender sensitivity is one of several resulting casualties.

## Summary of Gender Impact

Recent assistance and protection activities in Bosnia have had a mixed record in addressing gender issues. International actors failed to give legal protection to women who faced gender-based violence and other abuse in their homeland, in flight, or in camps. Indeed, despite the heavy media campaign against rape in war, women from all sides were raped throughout the war. Reports continued to surface late in the war about international peacekeeping personnel being involved in the prostitution and abuse of women. Although women who suffered from gender-based violence during the war could often receive refugee status, the process proved too much of an obstacle for many of them because few wanted to relive their horror in recounting their abuse to protection officers.

While some of the aid deliveries addressed the concerns of women and girls, numerous women's organizations and individual women in Bosnia reported a lack of gender sensitivity in the relief effort, noting in particular the absence of basic products for women. Although some international aid groups hired local women staff members and engaged local NGOs to assist them in their delivery efforts (particularly as the war progressed and aid efforts intensified), local women for the most part were not included in positions of decision-making and program design. As a result, most aid projects did not fully account for women's safety and privacy concerns, their troubles with taking care of dysfunctional male relatives returned from the front lines, their nutritional and health concerns for their families, or their own needs for medical and psychological health care. The most evident gender impact of assistance in Bosnia has been in the creation of psychosocial and microcredit programs targeting women which, as indicated, are of uneven quality.

Less evident has been a link between the work of aid groups and women's human rights issues beyond sexual violence. Although many assistance projects for women do not have an explicit gender perspective or embrace the goal of advancing gender equality, they have often subtly promoted the status of women. By receiving a large number of the positions with international organizations that are higher paying than local averages, local women have often been able to earn more than men. Although internationals still hire very few local women as drivers or as senior managers, women predominate in many mid-level staff positions.

While in some cases access to foreign-paid jobs has exacerbated tensions between men and women and between younger people who tend to speak English and older people who do not, earnings have helped women improve their material position. While enhancing the ability of women to provide for their families, the disparity in foreign wages may also create a backlash against women. In any event, without additional and reinforcing efforts to improve women's status in the family and in political life, the status of women will not improve simply because some women earn greater incomes.[33]

Capacity-building support of NGOs has frequently focused on

creating opportunities for the development of relationships across national lines. Women's groups have been particularly active in this regard. The Star Project, for example, has held many large meetings of women's groups from all parts of the former Yugoslavia. Still, Bosnian women's groups in their operations are rarely truly multiethnic. One exception is the group Zene Zenema, which was formed by three women who returned to Sarajevo from Belgrade, Zenica, and Zagreb. Its original focus was on women returnees and related legal and social needs, but it now includes many women who stayed in Sarajevo during the war and offers women's studies, women's human rights education, psychosocial counseling, and other supportive activities. Many of the women involved are in "mixed marriages." Unlike many women's groups in Bosnia, this group was not formed by outsiders and, unlike many groups, it is built around commitment to the work and informed by a deep sense of political conviction. Zene Zenema has survived on a shoestring, unable to secure major funding because it does not focus on microcredit or income-generating projects.[34]

Another positive example is provided by the work of the International Rescue Committee (IRC). Some IRC programs are specifically women-oriented and others are for the general population but also affect women. IRC programs have metamorphosed from the delivery of emergency food and shelter to longer term developmental-relief projects, including housing reconstruction, the establishment of microcredit projects, and support to local NGOs. They have integrated local people and ideas through many of their projects. IRC projects are run by local women. Although much of the mandate is imposed from the outside, local staff often have a great deal of input in operational decisions. The IRC program for disabled people in Tuzla is particularly impressive in its assimilation of and responsiveness to local concerns.

Some of the local women who accepted positions with local or international humanitarian projects found their attitudes and beliefs changed by the experience. Local women took away from the experience whatever was most meaningful to their lives. Some women found themselves immersed in local and international efforts to highlight that wartime rape and sexual violence are crimes and to support the efforts of the International War Crimes Tribunal for the Former Yugoslavia to bring the perpetrators of war crimes to justice. Many more local women turned their attention instead to more immediate local matters, such as the rebuilding of their families and communities.

The whirlwind of war opened a space for the creation of local women's groups that could tackle oppression and work for a more just society, sparking among other things enhanced interest in the issues of domestic violence and criminal procedures for rape. At the same time, some women in Bosnia, like women elsewhere, found themselves retreating to the perceived safety of more conservative traditions. Thus the impact of foreign efforts on attitudes and beliefs about gender in Bosnia was mixed. Many international organizations sought to remake women in society to reflect their own countries' vision of fairness.

"Not all societies are necessarily the same," Julie Gerte of OSCE in Mostar has said. "A society emerging from war has its own gender politics to negotiate in its own way and in line with its own history and traditions. One of the best things internationals can do is to foster and support networks of local groups and then to withdraw and let these groups decide on their own programs."[35]

## Kosovo: Uprooted Women and Children[36]

## Phase One: Abuses and Displacement through 1998

For purposes of analysis, the Kosovo crisis can be divided into two phases: the first through 1998, the second starting in 1999. A timeline charting major events during this period and the next is available in a related book.[37] The first phase encompassed most of a decade during which Kosovar Albanians experienced violence. Its effects on women were particularly severe.

### Overview of the Problem

For years, conflict has marked each day of the lives of the people of Kosovo. At first, the conflict was of low intensity, the kind of warfare that the international community could overlook more easily than the all-out wars in Bosnia and Croatia. Although the exact date of the beginning of hostilities in Kosovo can be debated, few would disagree that tensions were exacerbated after Serbian politicians supporting Slobodan Milosevic, president of the Federal Republic of Yugoslavia (FRY), revoked Kosovo's status as an autonomous province within the FRY in 1989.

This move subjected Kosovo to Belgrade's direct control and ushered in an era of draconian martial law and other so-called "emergency provisions." Kosovar Albanians were fired from or pushed out of their jobs; their schools were taken over by Serbian authorities and many were closed; and intense police oppression began, including torture in prisons, raids on marketplaces, and harassment of civilians.

In protest against the Serbian takeover of government institutions, Kosovars established their own parallel civil administration, schools, health care facilities, and welfare programs. While men held the top positions in the Kosovar Albanian parallel society, women played an active role as well. Despite extensive efforts, many Kosovar children grew up with substandard education, medical care, and nutrition, and with the constant threat of street harassment.

After the 1995 signing of the Dayton Peace Accord for Bosnia, Serb violence in Kosovo continued. After Kosovo was ignored at Dayton, many Kosovar Albanians grew impatient and began to support a new tactic of more aggressive and armed resistance, with the Kosovo Liberation Army (KLA) emerging in the vanguard by the end of 1997. In the spring of 1998, fifty-one members of an Albanian family were killed by Serb forces in retaliation for KLA provocation. Then, in the summer, Serb forces began a scorched-earth policy of destroying whole villages.[38] In hindsight, the 1998 summer campaign could be considered phase one of the war. Serbian forces planted land mines in border areas and shelled ethnic Albanian homes in the middle of the night, driving residents out of entire villages. Thousands of uprooted people moved across borders into Albania and Macedonia and many more sought refuge in other towns in Kosovo. Up to 300,000 people were displaced from their homes in this stage of the conflict.[39]

Prior to 1998, several humanitarian organizations were operating in Kosovo, but their operations were limited. The mandate of UNHCR, for example, focused not on Kosovar Albanians but on Bosnian refugees living in Kosovo. Mercy Corps International and Médicins sans Frontières (MSF) were among the few NGOs that managed on a long-term and consistent basis to provide assistance to Albanians throughout Kosovo, working very quietly through the Mother Theresa Society, a local Kosovar NGO with a wide network throughout the region. When the conflict in Kosovo first escalated in the summer of 1998, the amount of international humanitarian aid increased significantly.

Nonetheless, despite the best efforts of international agencies and the improved security brought about by the fall 1998 peace agreement, assistance did not reach the people most in need. Aid workers on the ground in Kosovo reported a shortage of emergency food assistance and continued difficulty in delivering aid, as well as ongoing state-condoned human rights violations against Kosovar Albanians.

## Assistance and Protection Efforts[40]

Women and children were disproportionately affected by the displacements. While men and boys stayed in conflict zones to fight, women and children fled to safer areas, yet most remained within Kosovo at this point. As in most refugee and displaced populations, an estimated 80 percent of the displaced population were women and children; over half of all families had at least one pregnant or nursing woman. The health care needs of this population, which hailed from the most impoverished region of Kosovo, were urgent and acute. The problems in Kosovo, explained in the accompanying narration story of an internally displaced family, were gendered, thus requiring solutions taking into account the particular needs and roles of women and men.

In many respects, Flora's family (described on page 40) was typical of the displaced in Kosovo in 1998. Most were hidden away in private homes, but most of the host families were beneficiaries of Albanian solidarity. They supported themselves and could not provide other financial help to additional people. Women provided for the needs of the displaced in nearly all families. Most had moved more than once. All were extremely afraid of detection by police.

Unlike Flora's family, a large percentage of the families from the Drenica region were poor and, in particular, most children in that region had gone without proper nutrition and health care for their entire lives. Thus, the health care needs of this displaced population resembled a population that had already been living under years of war. Protection efforts had failed Flora's family. At the same time, no international aid had arrived and it was unlikely that traditional methods of distributing aid would reach them. International groups would have a hard time finding them unless they worked through Kosovo Albanian humanitarian groups and, in particular, with the assistance network already established by the Kosovar Albanian "parallel society." An international group could offer support by transporting the child to Macedonia for her operation or by conducting the operation within Kosovo, but only by working with Kosovo Albanian groups to identify the family and with official Serbian groups that claimed sovereign rights to determine the ability of internationals to enter and work in Kosovo.

Collective distribution centers were never an option for families like Flora's. Families were extremely unlikely to come to a collective center, either to live or to receive aid. Serbian authorities were unlikely to permit a collective center for Kosovar Albanians or any other kind of international distribution without Serbian supervision and control.

## Displaced Children in Kosovo: One Story

In one of the walled gardens in Pristina, the provincial capital of Kosovo, Flora sits patiently on a stone bench fiddling with a picture book. The five-year-old's left leg is propped up with a large pillow and two wooden bars prevent her from moving her knee. A piece of a grenade has been in her knee for over a month. Her doctor cautioned that movement may cause the metal to sever her nerve permanently.

In the spring of 1998, Flora was driven out of her home by Serbian forces in Kosovo. The local hospital would not treat her, but a private surgeon offered to do what he could at no charge. It was not enough: the shrapnel remained. The best he could recommend was another surgeon in Macedonia, but fighting militia blocked the road to Macedonia. Her face pale with pain, Flora waits for someone to tell her what will come next.

The girl's thirty-one-year-old mother, Hedije, and fifty-five-year-old grandmother, Hajrije, take care of the other children in a small basement room: the newborn who arrived after the family had fled their home in Decan and who sits in a corner swaddled in borrowed blankets, the vivacious two-and-a-half-year-old girl who keeps the entire family awake with her nightmares.

Hedije was nine months pregnant when she fled on foot from Decan to the village of Iqmiq. It was there that five Serbian policemen gave her a ride to the hospital in Peja (Pec) to give birth. While she was in the delivery room, another group of police beat up her husband in the waiting room, accusing him of lying about his wife's pregnancy. Within minutes of giving birth, with the placenta still attached, Hedije was wheeled into the hospital waiting room to prove to the police that she had indeed been pregnant; only then did the police stop beating her husband.

The next day, she returned to the village, and it was there that she heard Flora's piercing scream that "just would not stop." Hedije made a makeshift tourniquet to stop the bleeding and waited for some neighbors to bring a doctor. Flora had her first surgery on the floor of a house in Iqmiq. The family used a horse cart to move the children to Pristina, with the women walking alongside it.

Pristina was the family's third place of refuge in three months. They had to leave the first two places because of Serb shelling. Both villages, previously 100 percent ethnic Albanian, are now uninhabitable and controlled by Serbs. They had first stayed in Pristina in the apartment of Hedije's sister, a tiny apartment across the street from the police station in the city center where Hedije spent all her time trying to hush the children.

When she sought medical care at the Center for the Protection of Women and Children, a Kosovo Albanian NGO, workers there suggested a room with a host family. The host family itself depends upon aid from a Kosovo Albanian solidarity fund to get by from month to month, so it could offer little except space and moral support.

This story is drawn from the author's interviews in Pristina in June and July of 1998.

International groups with large truckloads of relief supplies were likely to find the aid confiscated by Serbian forces, either en route or after the goods had been warehoused. Indeed, drivers for numerous groups reported difficulty in moving and distributing aid.

The international organizations that had the most success with aid delivery were those that worked with Kosovar Albanian humanitarian groups. The Mother Theresa Society was by far the largest group, with a vast network of distribution channels throughout Kosovo, including over one hundred clinics and thousands of volunteers. For eight years, the society was the lifeline for medical care, food, and other material assistance for hundreds of thousands of Kosovo families. Other groups actively aiding displaced populations included the Center for the Protection of Women and Children, the League for Albanian Women, and the women's rights group Helena. The center sent field workers daily into areas of conflict to work on emergency health needs and the League published and distributed ten thousand copies of a first aid manual.

One of the most urgent services Kosovo Albanian aid groups provided was transportation to hospitals for the injured and for pregnant women facing troubled deliveries. One doctor reported saving the life of a woman who had given birth in a small village without proper medical care: the placenta had not been fully removed following the delivery.

One nurse reported transporting a woman to the hospital in Pristina for a difficult delivery. Both the woman and child died after one week of hospitalization; the hospital reportedly refused to release the bodies for burial in their village.

In May 1998, the League conducted a survey of five hundred displaced families (approximately four thousand people) from the Drenica region. The term "family" was defined in the survey as related people living and traveling together. In Kosovo the average size of displaced families was eight; some families had as many as thirty-two members living and traveling together. According to the survey, 45 percent of all families had at least one nursing mother; 22 percent had a pregnant woman. The population was extremely young: 69 percent of the displaced were under the age of nineteen; 8 percent were under the age of two. The average number of meals per day was 1.5.[41] Interviews with displaced populations and health care professionals and volunteers indicated that the population had acute needs for basic medicines and medical care.

The displaced also had a great need for psychosocial counseling. The men who were among the displaced were frequently severely traumatized. Psychological support services for these men were nonexistent and thus the burden for their care rested with their female family members. "The women are forced to become the pillars of their family," more than one aid worker remarked. Women did not receive any support for the severe stress of caring for kinfolk.

Women also did not receive medical care and counseling for sexual violence. Some of the volunteer physicians working with the displaced had noticed signs that the women were victims of sexual abuse during their flight. Although the women were reluctant to speak of rape or other sexual abuse, some reported that Serbian forces (regular police or irregulars) had abused them sexually. The threat of rape served to terrorize the population of Kosovo. The threat of rape is "one of the reasons the Kosovo Liberation Army takes women and children into the mountains, to protect them," one woman said. "This is how they [Serbs] behaved in Bosnia." The international community did little to help with the specific protection concerns of Kosovar women.

In the fall of 1998, logistics coordination among humanitarian organizations in Kosovo was in disarray, with a few areas overserved and many underserved. In an "everyone for themselves" atmosphere, local Albanian humanitarian aid groups vied for assistance from anyone who would listen to them. Most international agencies continued to refuse to work with local NGOs (except when locals could play the role of cheap service provider), but instead established their own operations. The situation did not provide for adequate, equitable, or inclusive aid delivery.

## Phase Two: Escalation, NATO Bombing, and Aftermath

### Overview of the Problem

In October 1998, U.S. Special Envoy Richard Holbrooke negotiated an agreement with Serbian President Slobodan Milosevic to decrease Serb forces in Kosovo and allow two thousand unarmed verifiers into the territory under the control of the Organization for Security and Cooperation in Europe. The United Nations Security Council issued a resolution "welcoming" the October agreement and "demand[ing] immediate action from the authorities of the Federal Republic of Yugoslavia and the Kosovo Albanian leadership to cooperate with international efforts to improve the humanitarian situation and to avert the impending humanitarian catastrophe."[42] Although the verifiers were deployed, Milosevic reneged on his agreement to reduce his forces in Kosovo. Despite the presence of OSCE monitors, sporadic fighting continued. Serbs renewed their attacks on civilians as 1998 drew to a close.[43]

What could be considered phase two of the Kosovo conflict began when civilians once again became the targets for massacres. In January 1999, Serb forces killed forty-one civilians in the Kosovo village of Racak.[44] Although Serb authorities sought to block war crimes investigators from entering Serbia, international forensic experts managed to investigate the incident. They found that the dead were indeed civilians, not KLA troops as claimed by Serbian officials. The KLA retaliated and the fighting escalated.

In March 1999, the Contact Group (the United States, Britain, France, Germany, Italy, and Russia) brought Kosovar Albanian and Serbian negotiators together in Rambouillet, France. The agreement on the table required that autonomy be restored to Kosovo, a NATO (North Atlantic Treaty Organization) peacekeeping force be installed, the KLA disarm, and Milosevic reduce his troops in Kosovo. Neither side liked the arrangement. NATO threatened that Kosovar Albanians would be cut off from any international support and Serbia bombed if they failed to sign. The Kosovars signed the agreement, but Serbia refused.

In preparation for the threatened bombing, OSCE monitors were pulled out of Kosovo. Meanwhile, Serb forces and heavy weapons flooded into Kosovo. Holbrooke continued to meet with Milosevic, but the Serbian leader refused to sign the Rambouillet agreement. On March 23, 1999, NATO war planes commenced military air operations and missile strikes against targets in Serbia proper, Montenegro, and Kosovo. Milosevic responded not by capitulating, but by digging in and unleashing a pogrom against Kosovar Albanians. The international community was unprepared for the sea of humanity that rushed across Kosovo's borders.

The NATO bombing campaign lasted for seventy-eight days. During that time, Serbian regular and paramilitary forces swept through Kosovo, pushing more than 1.5 million people from their homes, many in the first weeks of the campaign. UNHCR estimated that by May 1999 at least 800,000 people had fled Kosovo for Macedonia, Albania, or further abroad.[45] While many men of fighting age were conspicuously absent from some refugee groups—they were fighting or had been killed or imprisoned—this exodus included a greater percentage of men than had the earlier displacement in Kosovo or most population displacements in Bosnia.

Many refugees were forcibly deported on trains; others left in tractors or on foot. Nearly all were stripped of their valuables and identity papers. Refugees gave eyewitness accounts of Serb forces summarily executing civilians and pillaging and burning entire villages. Women testified that Serb forces harassed and raped them; men spoke of other forms of torture and imprisonment; children remembered seeing members of their family killed.[46] Many men wandered across borders long after their families, having been detained by Serbian police or troops; many spoke of being tortured in detention and of seeing neighbors brutally executed.

The bombing ended abruptly the first week of June 1999, with Serbia agreeing to a peace accord very similar to the one originally offered at Rambouillet. The agreement called for the "safe and free return of all refugees and displaced persons and unimpeded access to Kosovo by humanitarian aid organizations."[47] Once again, the international community was unprepared for what followed. Within three weeks of the signing of the agreement, more than half of the 800,000 refugees in third countries returned to Kosovo on their own, making this one of the fastest spontaneous returns in decades. The early returns occurred despite warnings from UNHCR and others that people would face an uncertain security situation in Kosovo. Dozens were wounded or killed by mines and many returned to find their towns and villages completely destroyed. As in many postwar situations, the unexploded ordnance posed a particular threat to children.

As of August 24, 1999, 767,700 people, nearly all of ethnic Albanian background, had returned to Kosovo.[48] The return of ethnic Albanian refugees was accompanied by a steady exodus of the minority Serb and Roma population (estimated to be less than 10 percent of the pre-NATO bombing population), despite international assurances that they would be protected. By mid-July, 1999, UNHCR estimated the number of displaced people from Kosovo in Serbia and Montenegro at 170,000.[49] About half of the people displaced from Kosovo in the aftermath of the return of ethnic Albanians were children under 16 years of age. There were also elderly and very vulnerable persons among them. Many arrived with no possessions; some came by tractor and others by car.

Throughout the summer and fall of 1999, Serbs and Roma continued to flee Kosovo and Kosovar Albanians continued to return. By the end of November 1999, UNHCR spokesmen said, most of Kosovo's 200,000 Serbs had left. In addition, between 40,000 and 50,000 Roma fled from Kosovo to Serbia and Montenegro, displaced by violence from Kosovo Albanians who regarded them as Serb collaborators.[50]

The task ahead for reconciliation and reconstruction is enormous. International investigators estimate that Serb forces killed as many as 10,000 Kosovar Albanians, many in front of family members.[51] Other estimates of deaths are far lower, but the degree of destruction to land is undisputed. According to a UNHCR survey in the fall of 1999, 64 percent of homes in 141 Kosovo villages inspected were severely damaged or completely destroyed in the conflict, while an additional 20 percent sustained moderate damage. Between 40 and 50 percent of the region's schools were damaged. Only 60 percent of the water sources were drinkable.

## Assistance and Protection

Humanitarian organizations were taken by surprise by the magnitude of the humanitarian crisis, which affected men, women, and children. UN agencies together with donor organizations and NGOs met in January 1999 to discuss contingency plans for various outcomes of the Rambouillet-Paris talks. The best-case scenario envisioned an early settlement; speedy, peaceful deployment of international security forces; and a steady improvement in the humanitarian situation. This scenario never came to pass.

A second scenario, considered more probable and embraced by the major actors, foresaw delays in the Rambouillet talks and in the deployment of international forces and, as a result, increased fighting and additional displacement of the civilian population. This scenario existed as long as the talks continued. The UN humanitarian system found it had to serve a larger caseload under deteriorating conditions for delivery of aid. The international community erroneously expected that a political agreement would be reached without the involvement of international military forces. Acting under false assumptions as to the eventual use of force, the international community failed to plan for the mass population flow later that spring.

A third scenario involved the breakdown in peace negotiations, followed by NATO military intervention but without the immediate deployment of ground troops in Kosovo. Few international organizations believed this worst-case scenario would come to pass, at least not until March when the talks began to break down and the OSCE Kosovo Verification Mission and international humanitarian agencies withdrew from Kosovo. When the scenario become real, UN agencies and some NGOs quickly "adjusted their activities,"[52] ensuring, for example, that extensive stocks of equipment and supplies were not warehoused in Kosovo. Still, because the international community could not believe that either Serbian forces or NATO forces would carry out their threats, it failed to prepare for the mass deportation of Kosovar Albanians.

The United Nations Office for the Coordination of Humanitarian Affairs (OCHA) claimed that "the humanitarian crisis expanded exponentially, with no forewarning from any international political, military, or humanitarian source, and rapidly exceeded the available civilian response capacity of neighboring countries/republics."[53] Human rights groups had long reported on the crisis in Kosovo and had long forewarned of an impending disaster. Indeed, Serbian politicians had announced to the press on several occasions their plan to rid Kosovo of ethnic Albanians.[54] The international community, including most humanitarian organizations, chose not to listen to these warnings.

Once OSCE observers were pulled out of Kosovo and the "ethnic cleansing" of Kosovo began in full force, humanitarian agencies continued to underestimate the dimensions of the unfolding crisis. UNHCR planned for 100,000 Kosovo refugees in neighboring countries but was quickly overwhelmed when 227,000 people fled Kosovo in the first eight days. On April 1, UN humanitarian agencies issued the Donor Alert for Urgent Needs Related to the Kosovo Crisis, planning for an additional 350,000 new refugees or internally displaced persons to arrive in the countries or republics neighboring Kosovo. That figure proved to be far too low. A further addendum was issued on April 21 for yet another

300,000 refugees and IDPs, raising the planning figure to 650,000 outside Kosovo.

For all people of Kosovo, the impact of the international missteps was dire. For women and children in particular, the failure meant that they would be targeted for attack and forced from their homes, and that aid organizations would be unprepared to meet their needs once they arrived in Macedonia, Albania, and elsewhere.

The conditions for newly arrived refugees in Albania and Macedonia were horrendous. Little or no attempt was made to accommodate families. Macedonia kept hundreds of thousands of refugees in the no man's land at the border for days in unsanitary conditions, with little access to food, water, and health care. At one stage, Macedonian officials rounded up thousands of refugees in border areas and forcibly transported them to Albania and other locations. In the middle of the night, Macedonian officials cleared tens of thousands of refugees from these camps, herding them onto buses for Turkey, Albania, and other destinations. In the panic, children were separated from their mothers, families were forced to leave their few suitcases behind, and authorities provided little food, water, or information to anyone.

Once inside Macedonia, refugees were herded into unsanitary, crowded camps and denied contact with relatives further inside the country. The refugees who made it into Skopje and other major cities discovered a shortage of housing and assistance. While many Kosovar Albanian refugees in Macedonia lived in tents or other temporary shelters, many moved in with relatives and received little, if any, international aid. Given its own fragile relationship between Macedonian (Slavic) and Albanian populations, the Macedonian-led government felt threatened by the huge influx of ethnic Albanians; tensions between the two groups festered. Refugees complained about harassment from local Macedonians and of the failure of local police to provide protection. Humanitarian groups complained both of direct official obstruction of their work and of indirect interference, largely via cumbersome rules for registration of foreign businesses.

Conditions for refugees in Albania were similarly desperate. Due to the weak infrastructure of Albania and difficult geographic conditions, international humanitarian groups faced great difficulty in delivering assistance to the stream of refugees pouring across the Albanian border. Despite the assistance of NATO and other international forces, conditions in border camps remained poor. Many displaced persons slept in their tractors in muddy fields, unwilling to move for fear that they would be shifted to a worse location or be forced to give up their tractors, their only remaining wealth. Border camps were chaotic, with over-flowing and inoperable toilets and extremely unhealthy conditions for children.

Albanian authorities, unlike their Macedonian counterparts, attempted to accommodate all new arrivals. Nonetheless, they were hampered by their own constraints. They could not provide running water for the refugees in areas where no one had running water. Refugees lived not only in tents but also in abandoned warehouses, workers' quarters, factories, and in private accommodations. Foreign-run camps tended to offer better conditions than camps run by local municipalities, but in all camps, the heat, overcrowding, unhealthy water supply, absence of privacy, lack of recreation and fresh food for children, and other deficiencies proved to make living conditions grim.

At present, a substantial amount of assistance is flooding into Kosovo and specific attention is being paid to the needs of women and children. International organizations continue to debate how best to provide assistance in an atmosphere lacking full respect for human rights. Revenge killings and the exodus of Serbs from Kosovo constitute a core dimension of this problem. With a tiny percentage (less than 2 percent) of Kosovo's population now ethnic Serb, international organizations must decide whether they will continue the policy, now little more than a façade, of working to maintain a multiethnic Kosovo. On the one hand, international groups do not want to be seen as condoning Albanian revenge killings against Serbs or favoring forced deportations by any group. On the other hand, they do not want to be placed in the position of forcing Serbs to remain in Kosovo against their will, where they feel threatened and where internationals cannot provide protection.

However international agencies resolve this dilemma, they cannot ignore the fact that most Kosovo Serbs have left for Serbia proper, where living conditions are also extremely inferior. Some Kosovo Serbs are staying with friends and families; others are housed in tenuous conditions in more than thirty makeshift collective centers in all parts of Serbia and Montenegro. In November 1999, UNHCR stepped up its efforts to address the plight of displaced Serbs and Roma. It established a task force to find shelter in Serbia for refugees from Kosovo and rushed winter supplies to displaced persons throughout Serbia and Montenegro.[55] Logistical constraints, border queues, and poor roads crippled all winterization aid efforts for all populations throughout the region.[56]

## Summary of Gender Impact

Many of the gender impacts noted in Bosnia are evident in Kosovo as well, although the Bosnia experience at certain points appears to have strengthened the Kosovo response. Kosovo Albanian women had years to develop their own women's groups and to become active in their own indigenous assistance and protection organizations. They benefited from inclusion in projects concerning Bosnia, including many of the Star Project meetings mentioned earlier, the World Conference on Women in Beijing in 1995, and other activities designed to augment the capacity of Balkan women's groups. These experiences, combined with their long-term involvement in Kosovar Albanian human rights groups, have made them knowledgeable about the opportunities and drawbacks of foreign involvement, savvy about cooperation with foreign partners, and well versed in the operations of NGOs. Thus, although their numbers may be small, some Kosovo Albanian women are extremely well trained in organizing and in conducting social programs.

Ethnic Albanian women have consistently played a central role in the operation of Kosovo Albanian NGOs. While the Mother Theresa Society is led by a man, women doctors and nurses play key roles in planning and delivering assistance. Albanian women groups have their own humanitarian programs, which are effective at delivering relief. Their imprint as women is evident. While generally not sensitive to sexual violence issues, the Mother Theresa program has to some extent always worked on the needs of women and children, emphasizing early childhood nutrition. In their international requests, Albanian aid organizations continue to highlight the needs of women and children and to request aid specific to women's needs, including oral contraceptives, vitamins, sanitary pads, and pap smear kits. After their participation in the 1995 World Conference on Women, Kosovar Albanian women advocates have increasingly raised to donors their concerns pertaining to sexual violence.

Kosovar Albanian women's organizations have also emphasized the capabilities women can bring to addressing the humanitarian crisis. Women in Kosovo have the role of caretaker of their families, particularly in the villages. They are aware that assistance for children should be directed to the mothers and grandmothers, who will ensure that it is distributed fairly and efficiently. Kosovar Albanian women doctors and nurses visit displaced women from villages, counseling the women in the family as to nutrition and health care. Moreover, given their caretaking role in their communities, women can play an integral part in efforts to trace and find missing people and to reunite children with their families. Foreign aid groups that overlook women's strong role in Kosovar society will be less effective at reaching the children. Similarly, if they overlook the role of Kosovo Albanian women organizations and women doctors and nurses, their assistance efforts are likely to be ineffective.

Protection efforts in Kosovo have a gender component as well. As in Bosnia, reports of rape and sexual violence in Kosovo require swift but sensitive investigation, as do reports of bias and discrimination in economic, educational, and political opportunities. Women survivors of sexual assault have need for culturally appropriate psychosocial assistance, although social mores prevent victims from identifying themselves. For this reason, as was the case in Bosnia, such programs should be designed for women as a group, without singling out a particular group of women as rape victims.

In designing any response to sexual assault, internationals should draw from local expertise. Because women leaders in Kosovo are, like women everywhere, a part of the world they live in, they have the experience of the response to rape in Bosnia to draw from when organizing their own response. Some women leaders from Kosovo have been attending workshops and programs around the world on sexual assault in war and are particularly informed on the subject. Instead of subverting the plans of local women's organizations and using local women as cheap service providers, internationals should respect local agendas and involve local women in decision-making processes over the design of internationally sponsored projects.

As of this writing, many Kosovar women's groups find themselves overwhelmed by international attention. Much of their time is spent "servicing" internationals instead of implementing their own projects and improving their own capacity through their own training programs. The media and Western advocacy groups tend to focus on sexual violence. Albanian women's groups have identified wartime sexual assault as an important but not—it should be noted—a primary concern. They concentrate instead on women's human rights issues generally and on the involvement of women in reconstruction programs. Local organizations do seek international assistance with training and capacity building, but only if the programs are directly connected to real projects and real needs. Too many Kosovar Albanian women have gone through training unrelated to their own work.

While many international organizations have expressed a desire to involve local women in the reconstruction process in Kosovo, very few local women hold decision-making positions. Moreover, women are conspicuously absent from the high-level positions in the international bodies that control the fate of Kosovo. At a minimum, someone with particular expertise on gender issues should be leading a task force on protection issues affecting women and children. Instead of being marginalized outside the existing civil/military structures operating in Kosovo, this new task force should be part of the main power structure.

Similarly, while international organizations trumpet human rights as a main component of their work, the realization of women's human rights has received scant attention. Female protection officers with expertise on gender problems are few; women's protection issues receive only pro forma attention in most reports. International groups need to provide assistance in monitoring and reporting all forms of violence against women and girls and in establishing mechanisms for solving the problems created by such violence, including counseling, legal, and other forms of material support.

Effective gender training programs for local and international military and police should be established, as well as mechanisms to address any violations committed by such personnel. While some international groups have expressed a desire to address the issue of violence against women, their efforts to date have been of an emergency nature and directed at the violence committed during the war. The greatest need is for permanent mechanisms that tackle past and ongoing violence. Given the root cause of conflict, international organizations need to pay more attention to all forms of rights deprivations—social, political, and economic.

Many international organizations concede that their efforts for women are essentially assistance programs, lacking any significant protection component whatsoever. Those organizations that do claim to work on protection define it narrowly as physical protection, without approaching protection as the practical realization of human rights. For women of Kosovo, this means the realization of economic and social rights, problems that Kosovar Albanian women leaders have long sought to solve. Income-generating and skills training projects should be created that take into account local women's needs and skills. As in Bosnia, the kinds of programs that are most needed promote women's economic and social rights over the long term. The Star/World Learning Kosovo Women's Fund provides a good example of the kinds of efforts needed. It is supporting the training and ongoing work of women journalists in Kosovo (the Media Project/Radio TV 21), the locally created women's health and human rights projects (such as the Center for the Protection of Women and Children and Motrat Qiriazi), and other projects that contribute to the development of a vibrant civil society.

The very magnitude of the international response to the Kosovo crisis is a complicating factor. While there is a perceived need for cooperation among international organizations in Kosovo, including NGOs focusing on women, the reality on the ground indicates great duplication of efforts. There is a danger that, as in Bosnia, all organizations will establish the same type of project (such as psychosocial counseling and material assistance), only to switch at a later date to another type of project (for example, microcredit projects). This approach fails the population, which needs both. At the present time, for example, attention is being paid to reproductive health assistance, but few projects are aimed at the creation of economic projects for women. Both of these projects are needed, along with many others.

Another complicating factor is that long-term peace in the region cannot be reached without a regional solution that involves indigenous groups in long-term development and peacemaking. The entire South Balkan region will remain unstable as long as economic, social, and political conditions are degraded. Deprivation of human rights in any part of the region contributes to the insecurity of the entire region. This means that women's assistance and protection projects must be developed in Kosovo and in neighboring areas.

The refugee population in Albania brought international attention to the extremely inferior health conditions there and the utter lack of infrastructure for economic development. International organizations that planned to support the Albanian government in improving schools, maternity hospitals, and other institutions should not abandon their plans simply because most Kosovar refugees have left. Instead, they should support the Albanian government in its own efforts. At the same time, they should refrain from creating parallel structures that would compete with local efforts and they should consider projects for Macedonia, Montenegro, Romania, and other neighboring areas. Only if all assistance and protection programs are long-term and regional will individual activities contribute to long-lasting peace and justice.

## Afghanistan: Women Survivors of War under the Taliban*

Few places have focused world attention on women's human rights more than Afghanistan. International interest in the country waned following the Soviet withdrawal in 1989 and the end of the Cold War. Interest was rekindled, however, when a little-known force, the Taliban,

* The Afghanistan section was researched and written by Judy A. Benjamin.

captured Kabul in September 1996, driving out the opposing Northern Alliance. The military maneuver might have drawn little general notice if not for the new rules announced in radio broadcasts by the Taliban.

Women and girls were banned from schools and universities, forbidden from working outside their homes, and required to have a male relative escort them in public. A strict dress code required them to be veiled from head to foot. Men were affected as well. They were not permitted to shave or trim their beards or to wear Western-style clothes, and were required to pray five time a day. Movies, videos, televisions, games, kite flying, dancing, and music were forbidden. Anything associated with Western practices was outlawed as "un-Islamic." Violators were dealt with severely and publicly, with amputations and executions in the Kabul stadium after Friday prayers.

In larger compass, poverty, death, and loss of family has defined the lives of Afghans for two decades of conflict. The country is the world's largest source of refugees, with more than 2.5 million Afghans residing in Iran and Pakistan in refugee camps and communities. Like many of their sisters in other war-torn societies, Afghan women shoulder the brunt of war's impacts. They have buried their husbands, parents, and children and are profoundly traumatized by the seemingly never-ending power struggle that plagues their homeland.

Afghan women are divided by class, education, ethnicity, and tribal linkages. In addition, rural and urban women perceive issues in vastly different ways. Rural women follow traditional, more-conservative practices basically in line with the Taliban's edicts. In fact, some of the edicts affirm practices from before the Taliban's ascendancy to power. Yet even among rural populations the edicts are widely resented because they compel behavior that had previously been done of free will. Conversely, urban women—typically better-educated and used to Western practices—suffer a great loss of freedom under decrees that completely deny their previous lifestyles. Key issues for them may be of little concern to women who live in rural villages and represent the majority. Furthermore, women inside the country show a degree of resentment towards refugee women, who, they feel, haven't suffered as much as those who remained in Afghanistan.[57]

The ravages of Afghanistan's long war produced over fifty thousand widows in Kabul alone.[58] For widows, freedom to work outside the home may mean the difference between starvation and survival. Under the Taliban, widows cautiously negotiate the streets of Kabul, shrouded in the anonymity of the all-encompassing *burqa*[59]; many beg, relying on the kindness of strangers to feed their children. Widows fortunate enough to get their names on the beneficiary lists receive food rations from CARE or the International Committee of the Red Cross (ICRC), which distribute food to some twenty-five thousand widows each month.

## Overview of the Problem

While a comprehensive description of the political and historic context of Taliban policies exceeds the scope of this book, an understanding of the complex mixture of Cold War politics, tribal and ethnic differences, gender roles, relief assistance, and religion is required to discuss the challenges confronted by humanitarian organizations in responding to women's needs for assistance and protection.[60]

Afghanistan has been the location of wars for many centuries, but the first notable conflict of the last century was the Third Anglo-Afghan War in 1919. Under the leadership of Amanullah Khan, the Afghans successfully defended their country from the British, who wanted to make Afghanistan a colony. Although successful in maintaining the sovereignty of Afghanistan, Amanullah did less well in his attempts to Westernize his people. Requirements that people wear Western attire and attend coeducational schools were met with stark opposition from religious conservatives, whose revolts ultimately led to his downfall. Subsequent leaders who took control during the country's ensuing periods of unrest allowed the more traditional religious and cultural practices, such as the use of the veil for women, to be reestablished.

During the 1930s, Zahir Shah succeeded to the throne and his cousin Mohammad Daoud Khan became his prime minister. Continuing into the 1940s, they sought to develop the country and attracted Soviet and U.S. funding in the post–World War II period. Without adequate consideration of the real needs of the Afghan people, the Soviet and U.S.-funded modernization projects often failed. Ultimately, the more-educated Afghans became increasingly influenced by Soviet advisers. In contrast, rural Afghans were upset by the attempts to change their traditional practices. In addition to the urban-rural split, divisions developed between the conservative and moderate Muslims. Daoud's efforts to allow females into schools, for example, were fiercely opposed by conservative religious and tribal leaders. Similarly, efforts to free women from the veil were also opposed. Ultimately, Daoud, who had been fired, seized control of Afghanistan and declared himself president of the new republic.

During his presidency, the People's Democratic Party of Afghanistan (PDPA), a left-wing party, led the Great Saur Revolution, murdering

Daoud and seizing control of the country. The PDPA introduced sweeping economic and social reforms, many aimed at elevating women to the same status as men. Among urban women the reforms were more readily adopted, and in the late 1960s a woman was appointed in the cabinet as minister for health. However, the changes were radical and imposed without consultation with the rural people, sometimes forcibly. Urban workers who came to the villages to teach literacy sometimes dragged women to join the men in the classes. Such extreme actions increased opposition, with many villagers taking up armed resistance against the PDPA, which retaliated with killings and imprisonment.

Responding to increasing social division and unrest, the Soviets invaded on December 27, 1979, remaining in the country until 1989. Soviet reforms gave women the right to work, to serve in the army and police, and banned forced marriages as well as marriages below a minimum age. During the Soviet occupation and subsequent war, many Afghans fled to countries such as Pakistan and Iran. These refugees found themselves uprooted from their traditional rural lives in a patriarchal society, where women stayed at home and men worked to provide for their families. Religious fundamentalists who had opposed reforms for women prior to leaving Afghanistan often sought to continue traditional practices in the refugee camps. As a result, many NGOs experienced great difficulties in working on the specific needs of women refugees. NGO activities were impeded by lack of opportunity to communicate with women. In fact, many NGO workers found themselves targets of physical abuse for allegedly "corrupting" women refugees.

Not only did many male refugees impose strict Islamic practices on their families as a reaction to the liberalization that had been attempted prior to the Soviet invasion, but many of these refugees were responding to encouragement from the fundamentalist neighbors in Saudi Arabia and Iran. As a result, many women who had experienced at least some degree of freedom in the compounds of their villages in Afghanistan were now strictly confined to refugee camp compounds. Those whose husbands forbade them to leave the compounds (many husbands could not obtain jobs) often were completely dependent upon international aid, at least where it was available. Some women were forced to become self-sufficient, but while this allowed them to feed themselves, it also made them outcasts in the society in which they had no choice but to live. Others attempted to set up organizations to assist women (for example, in literacy and health skills) but they, too, were threatened.

Following the end of the Soviet occupation, Afghanistan found itself faced once again with the question of what should be done regarding the imposition of fundamentalist and traditional practices. Hope for peace soon faded, however, as *mujahidin* commanders and their followers fought among themselves.[61] The complex social and tribal mixture that characterizes Afghanistan gave rise to numerous fighting factions. These eventually coalesced into two main groups, the Northern Alliance and the Taliban, which are still fighting for control.[62] Until the religious fundamentalists took over in 1996, the country largely steered a middle ground, allowing citizens to follow conservative practices voluntarily, and on the whole preserving many of the social freedoms that women had under the Soviets.

During the resistance, fighters established bases of operation and training in western Pakistan near the towns of Peshawar and Quetta, where most Afghan refugees lived. It was there that the nascent Taliban saw its beginning. Young boys spent most of their early years in the *madrassas* (religious schools), where the mullahs taught a strict form of Sunni Islam. The foundation for the hard-line interpretation of Islamic teachings, which often consisted of rote memorization of the Koran, formed the platform of the new movement.[63]

The Taliban's takeover of Kabul in 1996 caused considerable concern to the international humanitarian community working in Afghanistan and, in fact, to the world at large. The Taliban, comprised of relatively unknown Pashtun tribesmen from Kandahar, surprised many people when it rose to power. It exploited the widespread desire for peace and need for leadership by promising to restore law and order. The goal of achieving a pure Islamic state guides the agenda of the Taliban, which holds the belief that the state should guarantee the personal security of women and preserve the dignity and honor of families. The Taliban's ideology mixes ultraconservative interpretations of Islamic texts with tribal codes and norms of conduct.

Taliban chief Mullah Mohammed Omar gained the support of a number of small warlords who put aside tribal differences in order to obtain control over most of the country. The Northern Alliance is led by Ahmad Shah Massoud, the commander aligned with political leader and former president Burhanuddin Rabbani. Thus far, peace talks between the Northern Alliance and the Taliban have failed. The UN and other international organizations continue efforts to end the fighting, although many Afghans lament the lack of serious interest and involvement on the part of Western powers to move the peace process forward. To date, only Saudi Arabia, the United Arab Emirates, and Pakistan have recognized the Taliban.

According to Mullah Omar, the edicts described earlier are neces-

Afghanistan

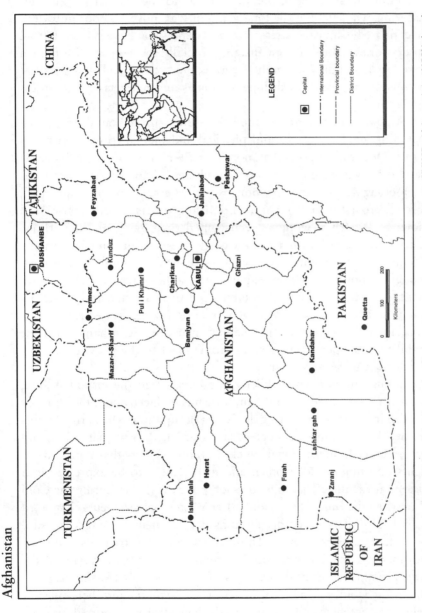

The boundaries and names shown and the designations used on this
map do not imply official endorsement or acceptance by the United Nations.

UNHCR with its permission. NCGIA through
UNEP-GRID, © 2000 Europa Technologies Ltd.

sary to preserve the honor of women. Despite the way the Taliban exerts control over women by removing their right to employment, education, and mobility, and despite the egregious human rights abuses it commits against them, the Taliban cannot be blamed for all their suffering. The effect of the long years of war, poverty, poor nutrition, inadequate health care, stress, fear and depression have created untold misery for everyone in Afghanistan, especially for women.[64] More men were killed and disabled in the fighting, but women and children were victims of the relentless shelling of homes and markets and countless land mine injuries.

Afghan women bore enormous hardships throughout the conflicts, including gender violence and physical and mental torment in many forms. One study reports that more than 76 percent of women's deaths during the war were due to aerial bombings.[65] Another study describes the lifelong trauma Afghan women suffer as a result of "multiple rape, forced prostitution, slavery, and other forms of gender-related violence."[66] Urban women, accustomed to moving about without restrictions, were devastated by the edicts. Severe depression led to some suicides. International health workers reported a number of women brought to hospitals after ingesting caustic soda—a painful but common means of suicide among women. Cultural stigma and religious prohibitions cause most cases to go unreported; some deaths are recorded as accidental. Depression also plagues men who feel ashamed of their inability to support their families. Some react to the stress by lashing out at their wives and children.[67]

While international publicity has highlighted the loss of Afghan women's rights under the Taliban, little has surfaced about the abuse of women in earlier years during the Soviet occupation, when armed fighters on all sides raped, abducted, and trafficked in women, girls, and boys.[68] Indeed, international shock at Taliban edicts that removed the rights and mobility of women and girls tended to be expressed in a historical vacuum. The stage for such policies was set during the Cold War, when the United States and other Western governments channeled million of dollars, often disguised as development assistance, to support the *mujahidin* fighters. Those shocked at the strictness and cruel treatment by the Taliban, however, tend to forget the behavior of the *mujahidin* and some of the customs of rural and tribal Pashtuns.

In the Cold War political milieu, the *mujahidin* and their quest to defeat the Soviets were romanticized, their efforts supported by massive U.S. government resources.[69] During that period, the international community not only ignored Afghanistan's gender and social policies but also failed to probe the wider effects of U.S. support of the "free-dom fighters."[70] During the 1980s, most aid agencies paid little attention to the needs or rights of women. Some even provided direct assistance to the *mujahidin*, an approach that had serious negative effects on Af-ghan women's human rights within Afghanistan. Abuses against women also continued during the anarchy following the Soviet withdrawal and in the years immediately preceding the Taliban takeover.

Today the pernicious poverty and other effects of the ongoing civil war remain the principal problems for women. Everything must be weighed in light of extreme deprivation. Food stalls in Kabul and in other areas display seasonal vegetables but people do not have the fi-nancial resources to purchase adequate food supplies. Most men and women are jobless. Families have sold nearly all of their household be-longings. The longer people live in such poverty, the worse their health becomes. Tuberculosis is increasing, with 70 percent of the cases among women.

Each year Afghanistan sinks lower on the UN Development Index. The life expectancy is estimated at 44 years for women. The maternal mortality rate is the second highest in the world (nearly 1,700 per 100,000 live births).[71] Family planning and reproductive health services are rare. One-quarter of all children die before the age of five, and lit-eracy rates for females are an estimated 13 percent in urban areas and 3 to 4 percent in rural districts. Some NGOs believe that the literacy rate has actually fallen in the past three years. Land mines injure more than eight thousand people each year, mostly civilians, including women and children. These troubling statistics help explain why women are more likely to talk about their desire for peace, health care, food, education, and shelter than about having to wear the *burqa*. To many in the out-side world, however, the garment has become a symbol of the ill treatment of Afghan women.

Notwithstanding that the generation growing up now has known only conflict, Afghans hope for peace and a time to rebuild their lives. Afghan women request information about civil society and human rights. Refugee women's organizations in Pakistan report an increase in the demand for courses in Islamic law: women want to know their legal rights in the context of their religion. They also study the Koran and consult Islamic scholars regarding their rights. Most scholars discredit the Taliban's interpretation and criticize its ban on education for girls, noting that it is an obligation to educate all Muslims.

Despite present trends, it would be a mistake to write off the coun-try as historically backward or unaware of human rights issues. Under previous governments, Afghanistan signed important international conventions such as the Convention on the Elimination of All Forms of Discrimination Against Women (CEDAW), the Convention on the Rights of the Child, and the UN Charter itself. Many Afghans value learning highly; a large number want their daughters to be educated.

The edict that forbids women from working outside the home brought additional hardships to employed women. Most families desperately need such additional income. For many widows and women heads-of-household, establishing a source of income is worth risking disobedience to Taliban restrictions.

## Assistance and Protection Efforts

International humanitarian agencies operating in Afghanistan have wrestled for years with fundamental issues related to women's rights and needs. They have failed to achieve consensus on how to resolve the evident tensions between protecting human rights and providing for human needs. Many NGOs and some UN organizations have adopted the rights-based approach recently promoted by UNICEF.[72] However, few workers in the field understand the distinction between rights-based and needs-based programming. Agencies face immense challenges as they try to structure programs to meet the needs of women and girls and also to uphold a human rights-based framework. The problem is made more complex by the fact that agencies are committed as a matter of principle to respect local cultural and religious practices and by the fact that Taliban policies differ from jurisdiction to jurisdiction.

Forced to grapple with the restrictive policies of the authorities, NGOs have charted their courses in different ways. CARE, for example, articulated a position of "principled engagement," negotiating with the Taliban to carry out programs but also suspending operations when its principles were violated. CARE suspended its widows' feeding program on three occasions when the Taliban violated negotiated understandings, using those incidents as opportunities to uphold human rights and demonstrate its principles to the authorities.[73] Oxfam and Save the Children suspended selected activities to protest the Taliban's edicts blocking equal participation of women and girls. Save the Children-U.S. closed programs in Herat when the Taliban refused to allow girls to attend school and to meet with international female staff.

Many agencies placed highest priority on keeping their activities functioning, seeking to avoid what they considered political issues. One such NGO is the International Assistance Mission (IAM), a Christian organization that, over a period of more than thirty-five years, has managed to survive numerous conflicts and social disruptions. While the number of its activities is limited and its approach intentionally low profile, it operates the highly valued Noor Eye Clinic in Kabul and carries out various community health education programs. Other NGOs, by contrast, have taken the decisive step of closing certain programs when they found no way around the edicts.

In addition to international NGOs, many local NGOs have worked with Afghan refugees, both in Pakistan and in Afghanistan itself. After the Soviet departure in 1989, agencies envisioned turning over assistance to Afghans themselves. Because of substantial UN funding, over two hundred Afghan NGOs existed by 1994, many linked with various commanders and local administrations but lacking community support. During this period a few Afghan women's NGOs were formed, often by employees of international NGOs. Afghan women traditionally do not form groups because their social spheres normally revolve around family and home. In fact, the concept of an NGO was foreign to Afghan women before the Pakistan refugee experience. While most Afghan NGOs operate from bases in Pakistan and provide services to the large refugee population there, many also provide assistance inside Afghanistan.

The NGO community in its various parts, however, reached little agreement regarding common strategies for assisting women and girls. In the early days of the Taliban, most agencies were baffled and conflicted about how to respond to its edicts. NGO gender policies were not clearly articulated or communicated adequately by headquarters to field staff, many of whom were on short-term contracts and without any particular background on gender problems.

One mechanism for discussion of policies and strategies among NGOs is the Peshawar-based Agency Coordinating Body for Afghan Relief (ACBAR), whose purpose is to coordinate and share information among the agencies working inside Afghanistan and in Pakistan. ACBAR had more than 150 local and international NGO members in 1999. ACBAR also provides meeting facilities in Peshawar for the Afghan Women's Network, a group composed of about forty women, most of whom belong to Afghan women's NGOs based in Pakistan. It also houses the Afghan Resource and Information Center, directed by well-known Afghan scholar Nancy Hatch Dupree.

While ACBAR played constructive roles for the NGO community, it faced two constraints. First, the restrictive circumstances under which agencies operate in Afghanistan limited NGO willingness to share information and discuss strategies with one another. Second, since the Taliban does not enforce the edicts evenly throughout the areas under its control, many NGOs have been reluctant to coordinate or even discuss day-to-day program activities for fear that they will lose certain privileges if too much attention is called to their work. A local official in one province may allow women to meet for training sessions, while his counterpart in the next province will not. Approvals from local Taliban representatives are also tenuous and not always sanctioned by headquarters in Kandahar. Frequent shifts in the Taliban organization at local levels threaten the sustainability of aid programs. Competition for funding among NGOs, while not unique to the Afghanistan situation, has also reduced willingness to share program information and data.

The confusion among NGOs was mirrored by similar conditions among UN organizations in responding to the same Taliban challenges. UNICEF, for example, refused to support schools for boys as long as girls were forbidden to attend classes. By contrast, the World Health Organization (WHO) positioned itself as fully cooperative with the authorities, particularly the health ministry. Different UN agencies responded differently to Taliban demands that only male staff members participate in negotiations. Such disarray was the subject of numerous missions from individual agency headquarters (a WHO mission attracted considerable attention) and of the UN gender mission noted in the following section.

NGOs themselves criticized the lack of agreement among UN agencies on policy and strategy. One close-in observer noted the impression among many private relief groups of "the apparent inability of UN agencies to coordinate among themselves, particularly the way in which the UN has handled the Taliban phenomenon, not least of all in the field of education and health care."[74] The Taliban took advantage of the lack of a coordinated approach within the UN family, as it did among NGOs. For both sets of actors, the Taliban delayed or refused permission for programs to operate, pressured agencies to hire relatives, and refused to meet with agency representatives, fully aware that such challenges would not provoke a concerted response.

Situated somewhat apart from NGOs on the one hand and UN organizations on the other was the ICRC, for whom Afghanistan represented its largest program anywhere in the world. The ICRC provided health services for persons irrespective of location or political affiliation, including frontline emergency medicine, transportation for wounded soldiers, and hospital management and training. The ICRC monitored prison conditions for both men and women and distributed emergency food aid to vulnerable groups like widows and displaced persons. The ICRC sought to protect access to beneficiaries by adhering to the principle of neutrality, which sets limits on the amount of public criticism of the authorities that it engages in. The organization avoided conditionality in aid delivery, an approach sorely tested by Taliban edicts that insisted on segregated health facilities for women.

*Innovative Responses.* Programmatic trends are not easily identified in Afghanistan, given the lack of transparency surrounding many operations. However, responding to the severe restrictions and limited options described above, agencies during the past decade have moved toward greater sensitivity to gender concerns and toward more creative, multifaceted programming.

On the policy side, the experience of working in Afghanistan has heightened many agencies' awareness of international human rights provisions and caused them to examine their own policies on gender. Reflecting the dilemmas experienced in Afghanistan and several other countries, for example, CARE launched a global human rights initiative and hired a human rights adviser who works with CARE's emergency unit to provide human rights training to its regional offices worldwide. The CARE family mounted studies of the impact of human rights considerations on its programs in four countries, including Afghanistan, discussed the results at a consultation, and moved to redesign policies, programs, and procedures to reflect its field experience.

On the programming side, agencies have tended to link programs like income generation and microcredit schemes to existing health programs in an effort to maximize each opportunity to reach women and girls by designing projects with multifaceted objectives. Some have creatively overlapped education with health training or community surveying and included such activities under health care programs—the area in which the Taliban authorities have acceded the most to pressure to allow women to work. CARE, which feeds over ten thousand widows every month, has expanded its emergency feeding effectiveness by providing health classes to women who wait for food distribution. Men are banned from distribution sites, making the areas an acceptable gathering point for women.

Health clinics provide venues for auxiliary programs such as health education, nutrition, child rearing, literacy, and skills training. Several agencies may share space in health clinics to provide training for related programs, increasing opportunities to reach women. Since there are no meeting places for women, venues for staff meetings and training are scarce and logistical arrangements to organize group activities involving women are complicated. Women are not permitted to ride in NGO vehicles with expatriates or with male drivers; staff must be transported in private taxis or buses. Women have to be home well before sunset and when traveling outside their communities must be accompanied by a male family member or *mahram*.

Given the restrictions on women's participation in programs in public places, some aid groups took the approach of bringing services to women at home. Terre des Hommes, a Swiss NGO, made home visits to pregnant women to provide prenatal services, although it stopped home visits after several months because the Taliban imposed too many restrictions on staff. Several agencies kept female staff on their payrolls, in some cases for two years, hoping the Taliban would lift the edicts. Each UN agency followed its own mandates. UNICEF withdrew support to public schools when girls were banned. The World Food Programme (WFP), the UN agency with the largest operating budget in Afghanistan, managed to keep most female Afghan staff but, as with other agencies, the women were not allowed to come to the WFP offices.

Private home schools began to appear quietly after the Taliban forbade girls to attend the public schools. Their formation was a community initiative taken because parents wanted their children to be educated. Some got started when parents pooled meager resources and hired teachers to teach their own children; others were formed by out-of-work teachers as an opportunity to earn a small salary. When female education and teaching by women was banned in September 1996, home schools sprang up. UN and NGO agencies responded by offering assistance: some paid teachers' salaries or supplied teaching materials and books; others paid for fuel to heat the classrooms, usually in private homes. The Taliban closed home schools in Kabul in the summer of 1998, perhaps because they were receiving too much attention and too many visitors. Local Taliban officials had known of the schools' activities and generally chose to look the other way, with several Taliban officials even enrolling their own children. The schools started up again soon but with less attention. Many home schools in rural areas were not affected by the closing of the Kabul schools.

The scarcity and high demand for reading material throughout Afghanistan prompted Nancy Dupree in September 1996 to establish a program of portable box libraries. Thirty-one libraries operate in twenty-one of the country's thirty-two provinces with a total of over five thousand titles. The boxes are placed in schools, clinics, mosques, and shops and are maintained by voluntary custodians. Although open to everyone, many women are users. Literate borrowers read to those unable to read. Women are able to go to some of the libraries themselves, depending on the location. When not allowed to go to the sites, they make their selections from lists. The innovative system, now operated by the ACBAR's Afghan Resource Information Center, bypasses obstacles such as the scarcity of reading material and the absence of public libraries since the war.

Some agencies now incorporate protection concerns into program design. One way to increase protection is by greater participation of women in program activities, an objective made more difficult by edicts restricting international contacts with Afghan women. The UN Guidelines on the Protection of Refugee Women and the People Oriented Planning (POP) tool developed by UNHCR promote participation as a means to improve the protection of women and girls. Since 1996, the Women's Commission for Refugee Women and Children has advocated greater implementation by NGOs of the UNHCR POP Guidelines in programs around the world. Helping NGOs with protection has been the focus of the Women's Commission visits to Afghanistan since early 1997.[75]

The UN system has been somewhat less innovative than NGOs in responding to the challenges raised by Taliban policies and practices. Attempts to encourage common policies through the mechanisms of the Strategic Framework Approach (SFA), a special interagency gender mission, and the consolidated appeal process for Afghanistan have not been particularly successful.

Launched in 1997, the SFA was an initiative of the UN Administrative Committee on Coordination, involving the UN secretariat and the heads of UN agencies, including the World Bank and the International Monetary Fund (IMF). The committee chose Afghanistan as the first of two pilot countries in extended conflict to be test cases. The approach aims to coordinate all assistance activities, including donor funding and programming objectives, within one UN-coordinated rubric. The multidisciplined, multisectoral analysis of Afghanistan's needs was meant to formulate one assistance program drawn from a common pool of resources and to make it subject to ongoing monitoring and evaluation. However, the SFA field assessment mission did not provide a mechanism to assess the critical gender issues that plagued every agency's work. Nor has the approach charted in late 1997 subsequently taken root.

In an effort to address the disarray among agencies, the Secretary-

General appointed a special interagency gender mission to carry out a gender review in Afghanistan. The five-member team visited the region in November 1997. Its report, which recommended a pragmatic approach to dealing with the issues and the authorities, disappointed aid agencies that wanted clear guidance to provide women with program benefits.

Yet it highlighted many of the issues already known by aid groups in Afghanistan and made three practical recommendations: that the UN hire a Pakistan-based senior-level gender adviser for Afghanistan programs to coordinate and guide UN agencies; employ more female staff at decision-making levels; and, with respect to the UN Fund for Population Activities specifically, resume family planning services in Afghanistan.[76] More than a year later, in early 1999, the senior gender adviser assumed her post in the Islamabad office of the United Nations Development Programme (UNDP). There is still no indication that the UN staff gender balance has improved, and the UN Fund for Population Activities (UNFPA) has yet to resume family planning programs.

Finally, the consolidated appeals process gathers funding for assistance programs within Afghanistan. The criteria for inclusion in the appeal include a stipulation that programs consider the needs and rights of women and girls and the gender roles of women and men participants. Donor pledges for the UN Consolidated Appeal for assistance to Afghanistan in 1999 totaled $112.9 million (U.S.), less than half of which had been received from donors by year's end. As with other countries, however, the appeal seems to be more a collection of agency requests rather than a consolidated strategy to advance, in this instance, gender and human rights objectives.

*Advocacy.* Agencies have been divided on the appropriate role for advocacy, vis-à-vis the Taliban authorities and the international community. Some agencies have linked their continued operations in difficult circumstances with a commitment to help change the restrictive local policies they encounter. Others have continued their operations but have eschewed engagement with the political realm. Still others have paired suspension of activities with the commitment of substantial resources to advocacy efforts. The effects of cumulative advocacy efforts have themselves been both positive and negative.

Even though gender is an issue that affects all international operations in all sectors in Afghanistan, some agencies avoided taking a public stand on rights for fear that the Taliban would close down their operations. They rationalized that it was better to provide some services than none. To stop programs, they said, would cause even more suffering among women. A few agencies made the decision to stop their work in Afghanistan because they felt they could not provide gender-equitable programming.

Although the public debate would not so indicate, gender rights involve not just the treatment of women. Restrictions imposed against men also raise fundamental human rights issues. As noted earlier, the Taliban forbids men to wear Western-style clothing or to grow their hair long. They are required to have long untrimmed bushy beards and to pray five times a day. Afghan male managers and supervisors are not permitted to speak to women—the largest segment of their client population. National Afghan male staff of humanitarian organizations may be held responsible for the behavior of women in their programs or when riding in vehicles; the Taliban may punish them for any perceived misconduct.

Ironically, it is the Taliban's own overt acts in violation of women's human rights that drew international attention to long-standing abuses against women in Afghanistan. News of the Taliban's edicts outraged human rights groups, whose actions, in turn, influenced world opinion and drew high-level attention to the critical issues affecting Afghan women. The high-profile visibility, however, did not come without controversy. Afghan women, patently uncomfortable in the public sphere, were embarrassed by the attention and voiced objections to campaigns that spotlighted their plight. They made clear that, instead, they wished to have more direct assistance and to be involved and consulted about campaigns on their behalf. Western gender views may in some respects be incompatible with Afghan wishes. A thorny issue for gender and human rights advocates is therefore how to help Afghan women without causing harm or alienation.

Emma Bonino, director of the European Community Humanitarian Office, visited Afghanistan in September 1997. The Taliban detained Bonino and her party for several hours after her CNN camera crew filmed women in the central hospital in Kabul. The authorities, who had granted permission for her visit, apparently became concerned at the size of the accompanying media entourage and detained her. (The mission had been warned that filming in the hospital was not allowed.) Bonino's well-publicized arrest was followed by a high-profile campaign, "A Flower for the Women of Kabul," mounted in Europe in conjunction with the March 8 International Day of Women. Whatever the benefits of these initiatives in terms of international consciousness-raising, they created difficulties for aid operations on the ground. In the days immediately following the Kabul visit, Taliban authorities arrested six

Afghan women employees of international agencies. There were undoubtedly less obvious repercussions as well.

## Summary of Gender Impact

Understanding the gender dimensions of the situation of Afghan women and reflecting these in programs presents a tremendous challenge to all involved. Interagency collaboration on crucial gender issues has ranged from nil to passable, but rarely has it been excellent. Where specific attention has been paid to gender concerns, some improvement in the status of women has been realized, particularly in access to health care and education. However, much work remains to be done to ensure equal access and services for women and girls. Efforts by UN agencies and NGOs to expand dialogue with the Taliban have opened the door to better communication with the expressed goal of improving conditions for women and girls.

The Taliban, motivated by a strong desire for international recognition and yielding somewhat to international pressure, have lessened certain restrictions on women. They allow women to work in the health sector and in other special cases. They have allowed home schools to reopen and operate throughout their territory. Most agencies, however, are acutely aware of the fragility of such tacit approvals. Human rights advocates continue to report abuses and to press the Taliban to respect international law and conventions. Flagrant disregard for human rights persists and, despite some improvement, there is no evidence to suggest that the Taliban's policies circumscribing women are changing. However, the gains are significant. Private home schools, home delivery of services for maternal care, and somewhat expanded employment options for women, while not a durable or complete solution, alleviate at least some suffering and provide a basis for change.

That said, the Taliban's edicts continue to present formidable obstacles to designing and implementing aid activities and to protecting the human rights of women and girls. To be effective, assistance programs must work within the narrow boundaries set by the authorities but at the same time not perpetuate the abuses inherent in the Taliban's policies. Agencies must take expedient measures as they deal with the unpredictable authorities, who remain largely without international recognition.

At the same time, however, a gender perspective must pervade all such activities, informing them with sensitivity to and clear understanding of the different roles, rights, and obligations men and women hold in Afghan society. Until peace comes and the opportunity exists to build a civil society where women can participate freely, humanitarian organizations and the wider international community may be forced to rely on short-term stopgap measures to ensure some degree of gender equality.

## Conclusion: Three Stages of Inquiry

The gender perspective suggests three stages of inquiry for working on gender-based violence and gender bias against refugees, internally displaced persons, and others affected by war.

First, gender-based or bias violence may be the reason for their flight. For example, rape and sexual torture may be a calculated part of a plan of forcing entire populations to flee their homes. Although men and boys face such sexual violence as well, the primary targets for such abuse usually are women and girls. Chapter 3 explains that rape and other forms of gender-based violence have occurred in war throughout history. Bosnia brought the issue of rape in war to the attention of the world community. In Kosovo, some women reported rape and many testified that they had fled because they feared that Serbian forces would rape again. The crimes of rape and sexual violence in Bosnia and Kosovo compounded the alienation because female refugees as women may experience social and physical persecution and shaming should they report the abuse.

Other forms of gender-based violence that target women and girls and cause them to flee include female genital mutilation, bride burning, forced sterilization or abortion, forced prostitution, and legal domestic abuse. Women and girls fleeing from gender-based violence need protection from their abusers and, should the conditions that caused them to flee remain, opportunities to start life anew through resettlement. One imperative, therefore, is recognition of gender-based violence and abuse as a form of persecution entitling the victims to international protection. Chapter 3 discusses the legal basis and mechanisms for such claims.

Second, while all uprooted people are generally more vulnerable to exploitation and violence than is the general population, displaced women and girls are particularly susceptible to gender-based violence and abuse—in flight, in receipt of assistance, and in access to help. Male refugees, refugee camp workers, members of the local population, marauding paramilitary troops and even international peacekeeping personnel—all have been known to sexually abuse women and girl refugees and other women imperiled by war. Such was the case in Bosnia;

the problem was even greater in conflicts in the Great Lakes Region of Africa.[77] The conditions of refugee camps and other settlements for uprooted people often permit such crimes to continue undetected and unsolved. Even if the crimes are reported, refugee camp workers historically have been ill-prepared to respond to gender-based violence, either in anticipation or after the fact.

Moreover, as illustrated by the case studies, rarely do mechanisms exist for coping with women's protection problems. Even when they do exist, women are often dissuaded by social norms from reporting incidents of gender-based violence and abuse. Women need protection in all stages of flight, including in camps and temporary settlements. Protection problems include the need for physical safety for women and girls; support for women and girls to seek redress for human rights violations and other abuses; and facilitation of legal protection of women through registration and status determination in their own names. The following chapter provides further discussion of legal protection.

Third, uprooted men and women have "different needs, vulnerabilities, capacities and coping strategies."[78] Many of the needs and capacities of uprooted women are illustrated by the cases of Bosnia, Kosovo, and Afghanistan. Assistance efforts should develop programs to support the different needs and interests of men and women. At the same time, assistance can "go beyond a recognition of the differences between women and men, and build more equitable gender relations."[79] Relevant assistance issues include such matters as provision for the health needs of women and girls; distribution to women of appropriate emergency supplies such as sanitary products; delivery of basic services by women providers; and creation of education and skill development programs appropriate to the needs of women and girls. All of these assistance issues can be worked on in a way that exposes questions of unequal relations and unequal access to decision-making. The international legal framework, discussed in the next chapter, provides support for such inquiries.

# CLARIFYING THE LEGAL FRAMEWORK

## Introduction

TRADITIONALLY, GENDER-BASED violence in wartime has consti-tuted private matters beyond the purview of the state.[1] Unless the state directly participated in the abuse, victims faced obstacles in seeking rem-edies under international human rights law.[2] In the late 1980s and early 1990s, advocates for women's human rights successfully pushed vio-lence against women onto the international human rights agenda.[3] A parallel development was the assertion of gender bias and abuse as a humanitarian issue: that is, one central to assistance and protection and covered by international humanitarian law.[4] These several victories un-derscored the duties of states and international bodies to take steps to prevent, and offer redress for, such wrongs wherever they occur—in public or in private, in wartime or in peacetime.

Recent developments are of particular concern to uprooted women and to humanitarian agencies that attempt to provide assistance and protection to them. In 1990, the Executive Committee of the High Com-missioner on Refugees, in a conclusion later endorsed by the UN General Assembly, made clear that ". . . all action taken on behalf of women who are refugees must be guided by the relevant international instru-ments relating to the status of refugees as well as other applicable human rights instruments . . . ."[5]

This admonition regarding international human rights and humanitarian instruments applies not only to states but also to UN agencies and other humanitarian organizations. Yet aid workers and policymakers often demonstrate little knowledge of human rights and humanitarian instruments, particularly as they apply to gender concerns. This chapter offers a comprehensive introduction to historical and contemporary developments, with specific focus on two topical areas of particular importance for aid workers: gender and the legal definition of refugee, and international recognition of gender-based violence as a human rights issue.

## Historical Treatment of Gender in Conflict

The earliest historical accounts of wars are replete with acts of gender-based violence. Rape and sexual abuse of enemy women are generally accepted as part of this story. Prior to World War II, Kelly Dawn Askin observes, "rape and other forms of sexual assault thrived during wartime, progressing from a perceived incidental act of the conqueror, to a reward of the victor, to a discernible mighty weapon of war."[6] At the same time, evidence supporting the existence of a concept of regulating armed conflict is found in most societies on many continents.[7] In ancient times, rules of war existed in many societies to limit and control conduct during armed conflict.[8]

Crimes against women, however, were not prohibited by these early rules. On the contrary, women were regarded as the property of men. The capture and use of enemy property, including women, was considered a legitimate goal of war.[9] In ancient Greece, for example, women captured from the enemy were considered "legitimate booty, useful as wives, concubines, slave labor or battle-camp trophy."[10] While the notion that noncombatants were entitled to protection began to emerge in later ancient times, the rape of civilian women in wartime continued to be accepted as a natural outcome of war.[11]

In the Middle Ages, *jus in bello*, or rights in war, began to take shape, placing greater restrictions on the conduct of warfare.[12] Despite some advances in the formulation of rules relating to armed conduct, "[m]ost of the restrictions applied only to weapons and treatment of combatants, not to the protection of women and civilians."[13] Women were still regarded as chattel of men; conquering armies were entitled to use enemy women in whatever way they pleased. Although some thinkers pressed for a distinction between combatants and noncombatants, the enemy was in general perceived as a collective body over which the conquerors could exercise unfettered control.[14] For soldiers, Susan Brownmiller has observed, the opportunity to rape was even a motivating factor:

In medieval times, opportunities to rape and loot were among the few advantages open to soldiers who were paid irregularly by their leaders . . . [T]riumph over women by rape became a way to measure victory, part of a soldier's proof of masculinity and success, and a tangible reward for services rendered.[15]

The mistreatment of women in war attracted international attention with the publication of Hugo Grotius's seminal work, *De Jure Belli ac Pacis*, written in 1623–24. Grotius conceived of a comprehensive system of international law that emphasized the validity of the law of nature quite apart from divine law and based upon reason. Although he retained the theological distinction between a just and an unjust war, he envisaged a law of nations based upon natural law principles and linked the concept of justice to humankind's social makeup. Just causes for war included the defense of sovereignty and the recovery of property. However, the notion that the vanquished enemy was a collective body that included combatants and noncombatants alike was rejected.[16] The rights of noncombatants, Grotius urged, should be protected. Moreover, rape "should not go unpunished any more in war than in peace."[17]

Grotius's work represents a milestone and its influence was linked to the growing recognition in the Middle Ages that wartime gender-based violence is a crime. Such recognition was not coupled with incentives for enforcement, however. As a result, rape and sexual assault in war continued unabated.[18] Eighteenth-century Enlightenment thinkers further refined the rights of noncombatants and the limitations placed on warfare. Rousseau observed that "[w]ar confers no right that is not necessary to its end," a notion echoed in the modern humanitarian law principles supporting limits on the means and methods of warfare.[19] During this period rape was "not necessarily committed as a conscious effort of war to terrorize the enemy, but rather as earned compensation for winning a war and a boastful reminder to the enemy that had been defeated."[20] Rape was not viewed as strategy to further war aims nor was it regarded as necessary to winning a war. Accordingly, it fell under the category of impermissible conduct.

By the close of the nineteenth century, states were beginning to take action on the subject of sexual violence in codes of conduct and regulations for armed forces.[21] These and other laws of war demonstrate the limitations in thinking about gender-based violence at this time. When rape of women was viewed as a crime, in wartime or peacetime, it was most commonly seen as a crime against the man: the husband, father and/or other male relatives, and against family honor. In other words, it was considered an assault on male property. Eventually, rape came to be viewed as a theft of chastity and virtue, but even then the crime was against the man or family who was entitled to the woman's chastity and virtue, not against the woman herself as an independent individual. The idea that human rights were women's rights, and vice versa, had yet to take shape. Further, the understanding that rape could be used as a weapon of war was unknown.

Although the foundation of the modern international law regime relating to armed conflict dates back many centuries, it was not until the latter half of the nineteenth century that customary principles relating to the conduct of warfare began to be codified in international instruments. In a series of conferences convened primarily in Geneva and The Hague at the turn of the century, states began a long process of codifying existing customary rules and developing new rules to govern the conduct of armed conflict.[22] The only provision in the early international agreements that applies to gender-based violence is Article 46 of the Annex to the 1907 Hague Convention IV, which echoes the language of earlier codes protecting family honor in providing that "Family honour and rights, the lives of persons, and private property, as well as religious convictions and practice, must be respected."[23] This provision is regarded as prohibiting sexual violence during armed conflict and, given early interpretations of rules requiring respect for the family, Article 46 seems to contemplate protection for women and children. Its presence in the 1907 Hague Convention was a significant development in international law regarding gender-based violence in armed conflict.

The practice of systematic rape during World War I resulted in the first effort to document violence against women in armed conflict. The War Crimes Commission established in 1919 to examine offenses of the laws and customs of war found that in the conduct of war generally innocent civilians, both men and women, were murdered in large numbers, women violated, and children murdered. Murder, lust, and pillage prevailed over many parts of Belgium on a scale unparalleled in any war between civilized nations during the previous three centuries.[24]

However, despite the extensive documentation of rape during World War I and the existence of international customary law prohibiting rape during armed conflict, rape and other gender-based crimes were not tried as war crimes following the conflict. On the contrary, nearly all attempts to punish war criminals during this period failed. While customary and treaty-based international law on the conduct of armed conflict existed in the early part of the twentieth century, political will to prosecute and punish violators of such rules did not. The rules of warfare continued to develop in the practice of states through international agreements and as a matter of customary international law. However, developments on the battlefield did not reflect the evolution in norm-building.

World War II proved to be seminal for the development of human rights and humanitarian law. Throughout World War II, women were subjected to gender violence, including rape, forced prostitution, forced sterilization, forced abortion, sexual mutilation, and other forms of sexual violence.[25] Nazi collaborators forcibly sterilized Jewish women as part of their attempt to exterminate the entire Jewish population and as a component of medical experimentation.[26] Japan enslaved between 100,000 and 200,000 Korean and Filipino women as prostitutes for their warring armies (see box below).[27] Japanese soldiers raped Chinese women in Nanking en masse; Moroccan soldiers raped Italian women; before killing them, Nazi forces raped Jewish, Polish, Russian, and other women in the countries they invaded and occupied; and Russian soldiers systematically raped German women.[28] These and other forces committed sexual atrocities against women and girls in all conflict areas.

Following World War II, the victorious allies established military tribunals to try those accused of war crimes. The International Military

## The Case of the "Comfort Women"

During World War II, 100,000 to 200,000 women were systematically recruited or kidnapped, brutalized, and forced to provide sexual service to Japanese soldiers as "comfort women." While 80 percent of these women were from Korea, then a Japanese colony, they also included Japanese, Filipino, Chinese, Indonesian, and European women. Each woman was expected to serve about thirty soldiers per day, for which she was paid little or nothing.

In recent years, the powerful testimonies and organizing strength of former comfort women and their supporters in the human rights community provided a catalyst for their own communities and governments in Korea, the Philippines, China, and Indonesia to demand an apology and compensation from Japan. In 1993, after more than fifty years of denial, the Japanese government issued an official apology along with compensation in the form of research and exchange facilities with the countries from which former comfort women were taken and funds for medical and social assistance. Though international demand for individual compensation continues, the Japanese response is a tribute to the strength and tenacity of comfort women survivors and the power of international collaboration among women and human rights groups.

One manifestation of the attention that women have drawn to this issue was the visit to Japan by the Special Rapporteur on Violence Against Women, the special investigator on gender violence issues worldwide who was appointed by the UN Commission on Human Rights. Her report condemned the comfort women tragedy.

*Sources*: Yuki Tanaka, *Hidden Horrors: Japanese War Crimes in World War II* (Boulder: Westview Press, 1996); David Boling, "Mass Rape, Enforced Prostitution and the Japanese Imperial Army: Japan Eschews International Legal Responsibility?," *Columbia Transnational Law Journal* 32 (1995), 533; Jan Ruff-O'Herne, *50 Years of Silence* (Sydney: Editions Tom Thompson, 1994); Janet L. Tongsuthi, "'Comfort Women' of World War II," *UCLA Women's Law Journal* 4 (1994), 413; Karen Parker and Jennifer F. Chew, "Compensation for Japan's World War II War-Rape Victims," *Hastings International and Comparative Law Review* 17 (1994), 497; Asian Women's Human Rights Council, *Primer on Filipino Comfort Women: Questions and Answers* (Manila, The Philippines: Asian Women's Human Rights Council, 1992); UNHCR, *Report on the Mission to the Democratic People's Republic of Korea, the Republic of Korea and Japan on the Issue of Military Sexual Slavery in Wartime: Democratic People's Republic of Korea, 4/1/96.* UN Doc. E/CN.4/1996/53/Add.1 (1996).

Tribunal (known as the Nuremberg War Crimes Tribunal) and the International Military Tribunal for the Far East (known as the Tokyo War Crimes Tribunal) represent a seminal phase in the development of international institutions to address violations of international humanitarian law.

The jurisdiction of both tribunals included three classes of crimes:

1.  Crimes against the peace: "planning, preparation, or waging a war of aggression."

2.  War crimes: "violations of the laws or customs of war" including murder, ill-treatment or deportation to slave labor of the civilian population in occupied territory, murder or ill-treatment of prisoners of war, killing of hostages, plunder of public or private property, and wanton devastation not justified by military necessity.

3.  Crimes against humanity: "murder, extermination, enslavement, deportation or other inhumane acts committed against any civilian population before or during war, or persecutions on political, racial, or religious grounds in the execution of or in connection with any crimes within the jurisdiction of the tribunal."[29] The charters of the tribunals held "leaders, organizers, instigators, and accomplices" as well as direct perpetrators accountable.

Wartime rape and other forms of gender-based violence, prohibited under the Hague Convention of 1907 and as a matter of customary international law, were included in the jurisdiction of the postwar tribunals by the explicit or implicit language of the charters of the Nuremberg, Tokyo, and subsequent military tribunals. Accordingly, gender-based violence could be tried under the charters as a violation of the laws or customs of war and in particular those prohibitions against the ill-treatment of the civilian population and abduction of the civilian population into slavery. Sexual abuse might also have been interpreted as an "inhumane act" constituting a crime against humanity.[30] These approaches were taken by prosecutors in Tokyo but not in Nuremberg. In addition, the charter governing subsequent military trials in Germany at the domestic level,[31] known as Control Council Law 10,[32] specifically included "rape" as a crime against humanity. Significantly, Control Council Law 10 removed the language "before or during the war," thereby envisioning charges of crimes against humanity regardless of a connection with the war.[33]

The concepts of individual responsibility for war crimes, human rights, and limited state sovereignty helped open the door to prosecutions of wartime sexual violence as violations against individual women. Testimony and documentation of sexual assault was presented to the war crimes tribunals at Nuremberg and Tokyo.[34] While the Nuremberg indictment did not include rape or other forms of sexual abuse against women,[35] the crime of rape was included in the general list of crimes in the Tokyo indictment.[36] At Tokyo, rape was prosecuted successfully as a violation of the prohibitions against "inhumane treatment," "ill-treatment," and "failure to respect family honour and rights."[37] Although the attention paid to sexual violence in the Tokyo trials was minimal, it has value for the prosecutions of rape as a war crime and paved the way for the prosecution of rape before the international criminal tribunals for Yugoslavia and Rwanda some fifty years later.

The war crimes tribunals at Nuremberg and Tokyo and subsequent domestic military tribunals were a milestone in the development of human rights and humanitarian law.[38] The trials provided a modern precedent for establishing individual responsibility for war crimes through international investigations and trials.[39] They affirmed that principles of international law included crimes against the peace, war crimes, and crimes against humanity. Although they were not prosecuted as such, these crimes could include acts of gender violence. The trials also underscored that a state may no longer assert that the maltreatment of its own nationals, however massive or systematic, is a matter exclusively within its domestic jurisdiction. The concept of crimes against humanity "provided that victims of the same types of conduct that constitute war crimes were protected without the requirement that they be of a different nationality than the perpetrators."[40] This meant that victims of gender-based violence were afforded protection from acts committed by their own government and its military forces.

Finally, the trials ushered in a new era of establishing international human rights institutions. The trials led to the refinement of the concept of individual human rights—rights people are entitled to simply for being human—irrespective of citizenship, nationality, race, ethnicity, language, sex, or other status.[41] The principles embodied in Nuremberg were to have long-lasting effect. During the first session of the UN General Assembly in 1948, member states adopted a resolution affirming the principles of international law established at Nuremberg, thereby placing the protection of human rights fully on the future international agenda.[42] The massive scale of human rights abuses during World War II and the vast refugee population it created provided the impetus for the formulation of international rules relevant to the protection of human rights and laws relating to refugee populations in particular. Many postwar developments are relevant to the position and treatment of refugee, displaced, and imperiled women and form the foundation for their legal protection today.

The problems of women in conflict can be said to fall under two interrelated legal regimes: humanitarian and refugee law, and human rights law. What follows is a summary of the salient features of post-Nuremberg development of these regimes insofar as they inform the legal basis for the treatment of imperiled women in humanitarian contexts.[43]

# Humanitarian and Refugee Law

## Treatment of Gender under Humanitarian and Refugee Law

Solid authority exists under humanitarian law for the recognition of gender-based violence. Humanitarian law provides for humane treatment of civilians and is generally regarded as binding on all states, regardless of whether they are formal parties to conventions. The principal sources of international humanitarian law are the four Geneva Conventions of 1949[44] and the two 1977 Protocols Additional[45] to these treaties. The Geneva Conventions classify breaches of its obligations as either grave or simple. States have an obligation to identify the commission of grave breaches and to apply criminal sanctions against the persons responsible for such violations. They also have an obligation to suppress simple breaches, although the means of doing so are left to their discretion.[46] Only grave breaches are subjected to "universal jurisdiction." That is, a court of any state can have jurisdiction over the crime irrespective of where it was committed.[47]

The prohibition against wartime rape can be found in many international instruments as well as in customary international law. Rape is listed as a simple breach under Article 27 of the Fourth Geneva Convention: "(w)omen shall be especially protected against any attack on their honour, in particular against rape, enforced prostitution, or any form of indecent assault."[48] In addition, it is possible to argue that rape does, in certain circumstances, fall within the definition of torture.[49] For rape to fit the definition under the Convention Against Torture, state action must be present and there must be some demonstration that the rape was committed for a deliberate purpose[50] (such as to elicit information or as another strategy of war). Alternatively, rape may be understood to constitute a grave breach of the Geneva Conventions under the classifications of "inhuman treatment" or "willfully causing great suffering or serious injury to body or health."[51]

Rape during armed conflict or other forms of sexual abuse may, under similar interpretations, also fall within the scope of Article 3 common to all the Geneva Conventions and which applies to internal conflicts.[52] According to common Article 3, all parties to the conflict are required to treat "humanely" all "persons taking no active part in the hostilities." Adverse distinctions in treatment based "on race, colour, religion or faith, sex, birth or wealth, or any other similar criteria" are prohibited. Article 3 also prohibits the following acts: violence to life and person, in particular murder of all kinds; mutilation; cruel treatment

## Understanding Humanitarian Law

### What is humanitarian law?

Humanitarian law is the body of international legal principles found in treaties and in the practice of states that regulates hostilities in situations of armed conflict. "Armed conflict" is the preferred legal term rather than the term "war" because humanitarian law applies irrespective of whether there has been a formal declaration of war.

Different sets of rules apply depending upon whether a conflict is internal (that is, a civil war) or international (that is, a war between two or more states or state-like entities), although they have some common protections and obligations. The main provisions of humanitarian law can be found in the four Geneva Conventions and their two Protocols. The International Committee of the Red Cross (ICRC) oversees their implementation.

### Is humanitarian law different from international human rights law?

Yes, humanitarian law and international human rights law have historically developed as separate bodies of law, with the former generally directed at the conduct of warring parties during times of armed conflict and the latter directed at the rights of individuals and groups in both peacetime and wartime.

Since the establishment of the United Nations, there has been a tendency to regard humanitarian law as part of the broader international human rights framework. Indeed, it is now well-recognized that human rights concerns often arise in times of war.

### Does humanitarian law deal explicitly with gender-based violence?

Yes, some of the relevant provisions are:

- Geneva Convention IV Relative to Protection of Civilian Persons, Article 27: "Women shall be especially protected against any attack on their honour, in particular against rape, enforced prostitution, or any form of indecent assault."

- Additional Protocol I of 1977, Article 76(1): "Women shall be the object of special respect and shall be protected in particular against rape, forced prostitution and any other form of indecent assault."

- Additional Protocol II of 1977; Article 4(2)(e) prohibits: "Outrages upon personal dignity, in particular humiliating and degrading treatment, rape, enforced prostitution and any form of indecent assault."

- The statutes for the War Crimes Tribunal for the Former Yugoslavia and Rwanda specifically include rape in its list of "crimes against humanity."

*Source*: This material is drawn from United Nations, Division for the Advancement of Women (DAW), *Sexual Violence and Armed Conflict: United Nations Responses, Women 2000* (April 1998).

and torture; taking of hostages; outrages upon personal dignity, in particular, humiliating and degrading treatment.

The legal prohibition against wartime rape and sexual violence under international humanitarian law is further supported by the two 1977 Protocols Additional to the Geneva Conventions of 1949. These protocols enhance protections for civilians in both international (Protocol I) and noninternational (Protocol II) conflicts. Although not included as a grave breach, rape is included as an offense in both protocols. Protocol I states that "[w]omen shall be the object of special respect and shall be protected in particular against rape, forced prostitution and any other form of indecent assault."[53] Protocol II prohibits "outrages upon personal dignity, in particular, humiliating and degrading treatment, rape, enforced prostitution and any form of indecent assault."[54] These provisions offer greater protection as they apply to all women in the territory of the conflict, regardless of whether their states are parties to the convention.

The other branch of humanitarian law that emerged after World War II is commonly called refugee law. In 1950, the United Nations General Assembly established the United Nations High Commissioner for Refugees to address the immediate postwar refugee crisis in Europe. As refugee flows continued long after postwar reconstruction, the long-term need for a refugee agency was realized; UNHCR focused on the transnational movement of peoples across borders in all regions. UNHCR has grown over the years and today is one of the largest UN agencies and the lead organization coordinating protection and assistance to refugees in many conflict areas. UNHCR is an operational agency with on-the-ground, day-to-day presence in many countries throughout the world.

The 1951 Convention Relating to the Status of Refugees and its 1967 protocol (collectively "the Refugee Convention"), set forth the definition of "refugee" and provided that state parties should cooperate with UNHCR and facilitate the implementation of the Refugee Convention. Unlike the Women's Convention, Children's Convention, or other similar human rights treaties, there is no treaty-monitoring body under the Refugee Convention. Governments and NGOs raise refugee issues by communicating directly to UNHCR in the field, at headquarters in Geneva, or through member states participating in the UNHCR's Executive Committee.[55]

The asylum laws of most states are based in whole or in part on the terms of the Refugee Convention. Under the Refugee Convention, refugees are persons outside their country of nationality who have a well-founded fear of persecution on account of race, religion, nationality, membership in a particular social group, or political opinion. Signatory states agree not to "expel or return [in French, *refouler*] a refugee in any manner whatsoever to the frontiers of the territories where his life or freedom would be threatened" by virtue of one of the enumerated reasons in the convention's definition of a refugee. Those who do not fit the definition of persecution, who do not fall within the limited persecution grounds, and who were uprooted but who do not cross state boundaries (the internally displaced) have little recourse to international legal protections.[56] The application of the Refugee Convention to gender-based violence and abuse has become a central concern of contemporary advocates for the rights of uprooted women.

## Gender and the Legal Definition of Refugee

One of the main debates on gender-based violence and abuse is whether a person facing such treatment could qualify as a refugee under the terms of the 1951 Refugee Convention and its protocols.[57] Given that protection under these agreements is linked to refugee status, the extension of protection to include gender-based violence and abuse, however constructive, would appear to leave displaced and otherwise imperiled women without comparable protection. Nonetheless, arguments favoring a more inclusive interpretation of "refugee" have had an impact on the treatment of all women in conflict and on broader issues pertaining to gender.

Influenced by the advances on women's human rights, humanitarian organizations have come to reject a dichotomous distinction between gender-based violence and abuse committed in the public and private spheres. Instead, they recognize that such previously accepted divisions should not obstruct the recognition of and accountability for gender-based violence and abuse under the Refugee Convention.[58] The UNHCR handbook asserts the view that violence committed by a family member or some other nonstate actor negates the protections provided by the Refugee Convention.[59] However, governmental action that implicates government authorities normally is required to fulfill the convention's persecution requirement of the legal refugee definition "where serious discriminatory or offensive acts are committed by the local populace, they can be considered as persecution if they are knowingly tolerated by the authorities or if the authorities refuse, or prove unable, to provide protection."[60]

The main stumbling block to recognition of gender-based violence has been identification of a recognized "persecution group" under the Refugee Convention.[61] Advocates for women refugees have made three types of arguments in this regard: (1) states should classify gender cases under one of the existing categories of the refugee definition (for example, religious persecution or persecution based on political opinion); (2) women who face a certain kind of persecution for failing to abide by social norms should be deemed "another social group"[62]; or (3) gender should be explicitly included as a ground for persecution.[63] The response of UNHCR to these arguments has been followed closely by many aid workers, including those who are not UNHCR employees or implementing partners.

The UNHCR *Handbook on Procedures* makes no specific reference to women. In defining "social group," UNHCR states only that "[a] particular social group normally comprises persons of similar background, habits and social status"[64] and that mere membership in a social group is not enough to substantiate a claim for refugee status.[65] The handbook does not set forth specific criteria indicating what would substantiate such a claim. The Convention definition indicates that, at a minimum, the social status must be associated with persecution.

The handbook notes that there is no universally accepted definition of persecution but that a "threat to life or freedom" or "other serious violations of human rights" always constitutes persecution.[66] It is essentially a matter of degree. While one action standing alone may not constitute persecution, a combination of actions creating an "atmosphere of insecurity" may do so. Discrimination between different social groups may constitute persecution, the handbook notes, if such treatment leads to "consequences of a substantially prejudicial nature for the person concerned,"[67] such as restrictions on the right to earn a livelihood, to practice religion, or to use normally available educational facilities.

Advocates for women refugees have pointed out that severe and systematic discrimination against women of a sufficiently significant degree may amount to persecution against women, thereby validating a claim for refugee status.[68] In such circumstances, women are completely left out of the power structure of their home country and are unable to vindicate their human rights at home. Such women meet the classic definition of refugee noted by James Hathaway:

The de facto uniting criterion [among refugees] was the shared marginalization of the groups in their states of origin, with consequent inability to vindicate their basic human rights at home. These early refugees were not merely suffering persons, but moreover were persons whose position was fundamentally at odds with the power structure in their home state. It was the lack of meaningful stake in the governance of their own society which distinguished them from others, and which gave legitimacy to their desire to seek protection abroad.[69]

Women who are unable to live under the dictates of the power structure of their home state may become targets of persecution by the state and may be unable to have their human rights protected in their home country. In 1984 the European Parliament became one of the first international bodies to adopt a resolution calling on states to recognize the right of "women in certain countries who face harsh or inhumane treatment because they are considered to have transgressed the social mores of the country" to be considered a "social group" within the meaning of the Refugee Convention.[70]

One year later, in 1985, the Executive Committee of UNHCR was called on to consider that resolution. The Executive Committee noted that many refugee women and girls are exposed to special problems in the international protection field, including physical violence, sexual abuse, and discrimination.[71] The committee did not make the approach of the European Parliament mandatory for all states, but rather left recognition of gender-based persecution up to the states themselves. "States, in the exercise of their sovereignty, are free to adopt the interpretation that women asylum seekers who face harsh or inhuman treatment due to their having transgressed the social mores of society in which they live may be considered as a 'particular social group' within the meaning of Article 1 A(2) of the 1951 United Nations Refugee Convention."[72]

In 1987, the UN Economic and Social Council chose the issue of refugee and displaced women and children for discussion by the Commission on the Status of Women at its thirty-fifth session. In 1988, the Working Group on Refugee Women, a network of nongovernmental organizations, held the first International Consultation on Refugee Women.[73] The consultation called on states to recognize gender-based violence and abuse as persecution and, specifically, to:

develop standards and criteria for the adjudication of asylum claims . . . recogniz[ing] the necessity to determine the extent to which actions of women . . . are seen by governments as resistance to political systems and/or religious beliefs; . . . and create reliable documentation systems that would include background information on the situation of women in countries of origin, and on the incidence of sex-directed persecution.[74]

Also in 1988, the UNHCR Executive Committee issued its second report on refugee women in which it advocated the inclusion of refugee women in the development of its guidelines specifically pertaining to women refugees.[75] In 1989, in response to the conclusions of the Executive Committee, UNHCR appointed a Senior Coordinator for Refugee Women charged with integrating a program for refuge women into the workings of UNHCR. That same year the Executive Committee requested that the High Commissioner provide at its following session a policy framework and organizational plan for integrating refugee women's issues into the work of UNHCR.[76]

Following the recommendations of an Expert Group Meeting,[77] the UNHCR Executive Committee adopted its Policy on Refugee Women in 1990.[78] Through a series of organizational goals, policy objectives, and operational objectives, the policy laid out the framework for the full integration of refugee women into refugee activities and programming to:

- Increase the representation of . . . female staff across all levels of all organizations;
- Promote . . . the full and active participation of refugee women in the planning, implementation, and evaluation/monitoring of

all sectors of refugee programmes, and of all entities which work in refugee programmes;

- Provide, where necessary, skilled female interviewers in procedures for the determination of refugee status and ensure appropriate access by women asylum-seekers to such procedures, even when accompanied by male family members . . .[79]

In 1990, UNHCR "affirmed the linkage between a violation of the right guaranteed under the Convention on the Elimination of All Forms of Discrimination Against Women and persecution for the purposes of the Refugee Convention, stating that severe discrimination prohibited by CEDAW can form the basis for granting refugee status."[80]

The most important milestone for UNHCR was the 1991 adoption of the *Guidelines for the Protection of Refugee Women*.[81] The guidelines, prepared by UNHCR and Susan Forbes Martin, then of the Refugee Policy Group, provide a comprehensive frame of reference for the issue of protection. Cautioning that "international protection of refugee women must be understood in its widest sense," the guidelines underscored that "the intrinsic relationship which exists between protection and assistance is particularly evident in relation to refugee women, female adolescents and children."[82]

Assistance cannot be adequately provided in the absence of protection. The guidelines establish procedures and practices for field workers and other personnel to sensitize the asylum process to the experience of women refugees, including education of administrators and judges, specific training on gender issues for translators and interviewers, and increased hiring of women in all aspects of asylum determination.

The guidelines also suggest changing the design and location of refugee camps to provide greater physical security, reducing the use of closed facilities or detention centers, and ensuring women's direct access to food and other services. While the guidelines have no formal legal status, they are to direct the practices of UNHCR and its implementing partners.[83]

The UNHCR *Guidelines for the Protection of Refugee Women* were augmented and refined in 1995 with the adoption of the UNHCR *Report on Sexual Violence Against Women: Guidelines on Prevention and Response*.[84] Although these new guidelines largely reiterate the protection standards set forth in the July 1991 *Guidelines on the Protection of Refugee Women*, they do so in a way that lends new attention to gender-based violence.[85] This report defines sexual violence among refugees, outlines preventative measures for stemming such violence, offers practical guidelines on responding to incidents, and summarizes legal aspects with respect to violence.

Some of the preventative measures suggested in the guidelines include establishing security patrols; providing protective materials such as fencing or barbed wire, particularly for remote refugee camps; assigning to the camps a greater number of female protection officers, field interpreters, doctors, health workers, and counselors; and organizing interagency meetings between UNHCR, other related organizations and government officials, and the refugees themselves to develop a plan of action to prevent sexual violence. As with the *Guidelines for the Protection of Refugee Women*, these new provisions, if systematically implemented, hold great promise for improving the lives of refugee women. Yet, field workers appear to have less knowledge of them than of the earlier ones. Few agencies contend that their field staff implement the Guidelines on Sexual Violence completely.

In its efforts to improve gender programming, UNHCR has also published *A Framework for People-Oriented Planning in Refugee Situations Taking Account of Women, Men and Children.*[86] This tool, originally designed by Mary B. Anderson outside the UN framework, seeks to help refugee workers to "ensure that UNHCR programmes do not disadvantage women and girls relative to men and boys and ensure that disparities between the sexes are reduced by UNHCR programmes."[87] The three components include: (1) a refugee population profile (an analytical map of a refugee community); (2) an activities analysis (identifying gender roles in community); and (3) a use and control of resources analysis (identification of what resources refugees controlled before they became refugees and what resources they control now). A subsequent UNHCR publication provided guidelines regarding implementation.[88] A number of organizations report using some kind of gender analysis akin to UNHCR's People-Oriented Programming in their work.

Also in 1995, UNHCR, in collaboration with other UN agencies and governmental and nongovernmental organizations, issued *An Inter-Agency Field Manual: Reproductive Health in Refugee Situations.*[89] The manual was intended to focus attention on an aspect of refugee rights that had been overlooked and to offer guidance to field staff in introducing and implementing reproductive health services in refugee situations. This publication was complemented by a specific set of guidelines for field workers on HIV/AIDS. In 1996, UNHCR, together with the World Health Organization and the Joint United Nations Programme on HIV/AIDS issued Guidelines for HIV Interventions in Emergency Settings.[90]

All of these steps brought UNHCR further toward recognizing gender issues in its programming. While some NGOs and individual state governments had already taken such measures, recognition of the importance of gender by the lead UN agency on refugees was crucial. The UNHCR *Guidelines on the Protection of Refugee Women* and the *Guidelines on Sexual Violence* provide a comprehensive framework for recognizing and responding to the needs of women refugees. They have exercised great influence on NGOs and states that had not yet done so. In this respect, the UNHCR guidelines and related programs have had an impact beyond the agency itself. To the extent that these provisions are applied to internally displaced women and other women in conflict situations, the guidelines have profound potential. The unanswered question lies in their implementation and extension beyond those who fall within the definition of refugee to others in need such as internally displaced and war-imperiled women.[91]

## National Asylum Laws

In addition to international human rights and humanitarian law, national laws protect women in conflict. Signatories to the Refugee Convention "agree to cooperate with UNHCR in the exercise of its functions."[92] This entails implementation of the UNHCR policies and guidelines on refugee women, sexual violence, HIV/AIDS, and the like:

[N]ational laws and policies determine what legal status an individual receives, where she will live, and what assistance is provided . . . many of the offenses against women, such as rape and physical attack, are punishable by national law. A further legal framework, within the national framework, is provided by the legal codes and processes adopted for internal use in refugee camps.[93]

States have watched closely the developments in gender approaches to refugee status. Some have kept pace with these changes, while others have not. Canada in 1993 became the first country in the world to recognize gender-based persecution as a ground for refugee status as an official countrywide policy.[94] Significantly, the guidelines issued by the Canadian Immigration and Refugee Board make no distinction between public and private violence:

A subgroup of women can be identified by reference to the fact of their exposure or vulnerability for physical, cultural or other reasons, to violence, including domestic violence, in an environment that denies them protection. These women face violence amounting to persecution because of their particular vulnerability as women in their societies and because they are so unprotected.[95]

To prove gender-based persecution under the Canadian guidelines, an applicant must demonstrate that

she has a genuine fear of harm, that her gender is the reason for the harm, that the harm is sufficiently serious to amount to persecution, that there is a reasonable possibility for the feared persecution to occur if she is to return to her country of origin and she has no reasonable expectation of adequate national protection.[96]

Recognizing that women may suffer different forms of persecution than men, the Canadian guidelines set forth four categories of persecution directed at women: (1) persecution under the 1951 Refugee Convention grounds "in similar circumstances as men"; (2) persecution related to kinship; (3) persecution based on gender discrimination; and (4) persecution as a "consequence for failing to conform to, or of transgressing, gender-discriminating religious or customary laws and practices in their country of origin."[97]

In 1995, the United States opened the door to similar claims by adopting Immigration and Naturalization Service (INS) considerations that permitted immigration officers to consider that women may face gender persecution.[98] Its document defined gender persecution as "sexual abuse, rape, infanticide, genital mutilation, forced marriage, slavery, domestic violence, and forced abortion"[99] or other harm inflicted upon a woman because she belongs to a social group composed of women. INS cautioned that "[t]he appearance of sexual violence in a claim should not lead adjudicators to conclude automatically that the claim is an instance of purely personal harm."[100] In other words, one cannot claim that sexual violence is inherently "private" and "off limits" to government scrutiny.

Claims for gender-based persecution are to be treated in the U.S. context as any other claims. "The form of harm or punishment may be selected because of the gender of the victim, but the analysis of the claim should not vary based on the gender of the victim."[101] A claim may qualify as gender persecution if the applicant demonstrates that the act against her is not purely personal, that the harm constitutes "persecution" as otherwise defined by the INS, and the danger of harm exists throughout the home country. Nonetheless, in most incidents of gender-based violence in which women receive asylum in the United

States, the grounds are not gender alone but rather something else in addition to gender (such as political persecution).

The steps taken by Canada and the United States to recognize gender-based persecution as grounds for asylum add further weight to the argument that protection officers should pay more attention to gender issues. The implications in the field of state practices with regard to gender claims for asylum have yet to be fully explored.

## Human Rights Law

### Treatment of Gender under Human Rights Law

Principles of individual human rights promoted by the trials at Nuremberg were detailed in the United Nations Charter (1945)[102] and the Universal Declaration of Human Rights (UDHR) (1948).[103] Among its guarantees, the UDHR recognizes the right to seek asylum from persecution and recognizes the right to freedom from torture and inhuman, cruel, or degrading treatment or punishment. Article 12 of the UDHR provides that "[n]o one shall be subjected to arbitrary interference with his privacy, family, home or correspondence, nor to attacks upon his honour and reputation" and, further, states that "[e]veryone has the right to the protection of the law against such interference or attacks." Despite the sexist language of the day, all of these are core protections for women and form the point of departure for a consideration of the human rights protections accorded to women in conflict situations.

Prohibitions against discrimination based on sex are found both in the UN Charter and UDHR and in general international human rights treaties, including the International Covenant on Civil and Political Rights (ICCPR)[104] and the International Covenant on Social, Economic and Cultural Rights (ICESCR).[105] In addition, women's rights are protected under specific regional human rights laws (most prominently the Convention on the Elimination of All Forms of Discrimination Against Women (CEDAW), also referred to as "the Women's Convention"), defined in various regional human rights treaties and implemented by regional bodies. These international and regional instruments are often cited as authority for the proposition that women and men are equally entitled to all civil, political, economic, social, and cultural rights, including the right to life, liberty, and security of the person, and the right to be free from torture and other cruel, inhuman, or degrading treatment.

The Women's Convention,[106] the main human rights instrument

## Understanding the Women's Convention

### What does it prohibit?

The Convention on the Elimination of All Forms of Discrimination Against Women prohibits all forms of discrimination against women, not just the elimination of "sex discrimination." Instead of simply calling for gender neutrality (the same treatment for men and women), the convention takes the more assertive approach of prohibiting practices that perpetuate women's inequality. The convention applies to both intentional discrimination and acts that have a discriminatory effect.

### How does it define discrimination?

Article 1 defines discrimination as "any distinction, exclusion or restriction made on the basis of sex which has the purpose or effect of impairing or nullifying the recognition of enjoyment or exercise by women, irrespective of their marital status, on a basis of equality of men and women, of human rights and fundamental freedoms in the political, social, cultural, civil or any other field." This definition includes what could be considered the private sphere of family as well as the public sphere of political life.

### What must states do to eliminate discrimination against women?

States that are parties to the convention agree not only to address individual instances of abuse and bias but to take "all appropriate means" to achieve equality for men and women. Article 2 states that, among other measures, states agree "[t]o establish legal protection of the rights of women on an equal basis with men and to ensure through competent national tribunals and other public institutions the effective protection of women against any act of discrimination; [t]o refrain from engaging in any act or practice of discrimination against women and to ensure that public authorities and institutions shall act in conformity with this obligation; [t]o take all appropriate measures to eliminate discrimination against women by any person, organization or enterprise; and [t]o take all appropriate measures, including legislation, to modify or abolish existing

laws, regulations, customs and practices which constitute discrimination against women . . ."

### Can "culture" be used as an excuse for discrimination?

No. In addition to the provisions of Article 2 stated above,
Article 5 affirms that states that are parties to the treaty shall
"take all appropriate measures" to "modify the social and cultural patterns of conduct of men and women, with a view to
achieving the elimination of prejudices and customary and all
other practices which are based on the idea of the inferiority
or the superiority of either of the sexes or a stereotyped role
for men and women." These provisions apply to traditional
practices that harm the lives and health of women and girls,
including those practices that trigger flight, such as female genital mutilation.

*Source*: Women, Law, and Development and Human Rights Watch
(Women's Rights Project), *Women's Human Rights Step by Step* (Wash-
ington, D.C.: Women, Law, and Development and Human Rights
Watch, 1997), 36–37.

addressing the human rights of women, imposes on states an obligation
to abolish discriminatory laws and to take other measures to promote
the status of women. Although uprooted women are not explicitly mentioned, the Women's Convention does apply to all women. Thus
principles set forth in the Women's Convention should be regarded as
guidelines for all policies and programs established for refugee, displaced,
and war-imperiled women. Article 1 of the Women's Convention defines discrimination broadly as any "distinction, exclusion or restriction
made on the basis of sex which has the effect or purpose of impairing or
nullifying the recognition, enjoyment or exercise by women . . . of human rights and fundamental freedoms" in all aspects of life.[107] This
provision applies directly to humanitarian activities undertaken by states
that are parties to the Women's Convention.

The Committee on the Elimination of Discrimination Against
Women is the monitoring body of the Women's Convention. The committee is composed of twenty-three experts serving in their personal
capacities. Their main task is to consider state compliance with the convention, largely through review of periodic country reports. The

committee examines country reports during their annual meetings. Although NGOs have no formal right to submit reports, the committee does, in fact, receive and consider "alternative country reports" from NGOs. Apart from submitting reports and commentary directly to the committee, NGOs have no right to submit individual complaints. While many NGOs and some governments have pushed for adoption of an optional protocol to the Women's Convention that would create individual and interstate complaint procedures, as of this writing that protocol has failed to garner sufficient support.

Another important international legal instrument for raising gender issues is the Convention on the Rights of the Child[108] (the "Children's Convention"). Unlike the Women's Convention, it specifically recognizes the right of child refugees to "receive appropriate protection and humanitarian assistance" (Article 22). The Children's Convention also requires that state parties "respect and ensure the rights set forth in the present convention without discrimination of any kind, irrespective of the child's or his or her parent's or legal guardian's race, colour, sex, language, religion, political or other opinion, national, ethnic or social origin, property, disability, birth or other status" (Article 62). Sex discrimination is clearly prohibited under this provision; refugee and immigration status are implicitly included as well.

The Committee on the Rights of the Child (CRC) is the monitoring body for the Children's Convention. As under the Women's Convention, the Children's Convention does not permit the CRC to decide individual complaints; its primary function is to review state reports on their own compliance. Nonetheless, the CRC can and does solicit information from UN agencies (such as UNICEF, which is the primary UN focal point for children's rights and needs) and NGOs. In addition, the CRC relies heavily on experts drawn from the NGO community.

International human rights instruments provide a framework for carrying out protection and assistance activities on behalf of women in conflict.[109] Humanitarian agencies have not fully used this framework, as they often labor under the impression that human rights work and the provision of emergency assistance are separate domains. To be sure, assistance groups might jeopardize their own operational capacities should they vociferously publicize human rights violations. But using the human rights rubric as a normative framework for humanitarian goals does not mean becoming a human rights advocacy group. It does, however, entail recognizing the ways in which humanitarian action contributes to or hinders the realization of human rights and the ways in which human rights principles support humanitarian action. The failure of aid groups to do so has resulted in the following roadblocks to progress on gender issues.[110]

- Continued acceptance of a public/private dichotomy. Sexual abuse tends to be relegated to the private sphere, where it is not adequately acknowledged and states are not held accountable for it.

- Sexual and reproductive rights are not fully recognized. States claim no obligation to respect the sexual and reproductive rights of women and men. When women experience violations of their reproductive rights, they are likely to have no recourse for the abuse.

- Misapplied respect for culture. States use "culture" as an excuse to justify violations of women's human rights. As the World Health Organization and UNICEF have pointed out, however, "People will change their behavior when they understand the hazards and indignity of harmful practices and when they realize that it is possible to give up harmful cultural practices without giving up meaningful aspects of their culture."[111]

- Undeveloped mechanisms for enforcement of social and economic rights. Many of the violations women experience are in conflict with recognized social, economic, and cultural rights. Enforcement mechanisms for such rights, however, are weaker than those for civil and political rights.

- Undeveloped mechanisms for enforcement of women's human rights. The enforcement mechanisms for women's human rights are among the weakest in the entire international human rights system. CEDAW does not yet have an optional protocol that would create a procedure for individual complaints from victims of violations.

Further work is needed in developing responses to these constraints. Through their work, humanitarian organizations could take steps to work on such obstacles, challenging and even denouncing difficulties where appropriate and taking corrective action where feasible. Aid agencies should continue to tackle issues for which there are no effective enforcement mechanisms, adjusting their practices where appropriate to work around the lack of enforcement. At the very least, aid agencies should consider how to avoid contributing to the perpetuation of these problems.

## Recognition of Gender Violence as a Violation of Women's Rights

Recognizing gender violence against women as a human rights concern was necessary in order to trigger international legal procedures and to focus government attention on gender issues. Slow in coming, this recognition was only recently achieved. One of the first references to gender and conflict was in 1969, when the UN Commission on the Status of Women (CSW) began to consider whether "special protection should be accorded to vulnerable groups, namely women and children, during armed conflict and emergency situations."[112] In 1974, the UN General Assembly adopted a Declaration on the Protection of Women and Children in Emergency and Armed Conflict.[113] The declaration stresses that the roles women play as mothers and caregivers entitle them to special protection, but it fails to recognize gender-based violence altogether.

International documents throughout the 1980s tended to group women and children as a "vulnerable category" in conflict situations, and thereby entitled to special protection. Women were not seen as individuals beyond their role as mothers, and sexual violence in armed conflict was largely unrecognized.[114] The situation began changing slowly in 1985 when the World Conference on Women, meeting in Nairobi, adopted Forward Looking Strategies for Advancement of Women, which specifically referred to physical abuse against women in armed conflict and drew attention to the concerns of refugee women.[115]

The next milestone came in 1992 when the Committee on the Elimination of Discrimination Against Women, the body responsible for monitoring the implementation of CEDAW, reaffirmed that both private and public violence against women is indeed a human rights violation. Recommendation 19 adopted by the CEDAW establishes the links between violence against women and gender discrimination:

Violence against women is both a consequence of systematic discrimination against women in public and private life, and a means by which constraints on women's rights are reinforced. Women are vulnerable because of disabilities imposed on them in economic, social, cultural, civil and political life and violence impairs the extent to which they are able to exercise de jure rights.

The breakdown of the public/private divide in Article 19 furthered the goals of advocates to recognize harms committed to women in both wartime and peacetime.

Growing attention to women's rights was spurred by developments in the conflicts themselves. Reports of systematic rape of women in

## From Vienna to Beijing:
## The Petition Campaign for Women's Human Rights

A petition drive launched during the 16 Days of Activism Against Gender Violence in 1991 is one model of how women used the 1993 World Conference on Human Rights in Vienna and the 1995 Fourth World Conference on Women to move women's human rights to center stage.

The petition called on the UN to include women's rights as human rights on the agenda of the Vienna Conference and specifically to recognize violence against women as a violation of human rights. Women in 124 countries worked to gather hundreds of thousands of signatures, which were delivered to the floor of the official proceedings of the World Conference on Human Rights in Vienna. A follow-up petition called on the UN to report on its enforcement of commitments made in Vienna during the Fourth World Conference on Women in Beijing in 1995. This final petition was delivered to the former UN High Commissioner for Human Rights, José Ayala-Lasso, at the World Conference on Women in Beijing.

*Source:* Julie Mertus with Nancy Flowers and Mallika Dutt, *Local Action/Global Change: Learning About the Human Rights of Women and Girls* (New York: UNIFEM and the Center for Women's Global Leadership, 1999).

Bosnia-Herzegovina, in particular of Muslim women by Serbian forces, surfaced in 1992. On December 18, 1992, the UN Security Council adopted a UN resolution condemning "massive and organized detention and rape of women."[116] These and other UN resolutions, nongovernmental and governmental reports, and journalistic accounts attracted worldwide attention to the plight of women in conflict.

Reports of gender-based violence from Bosnia galvanized human rights advocates at the 1993 World Conference on Human Rights in Vienna. Including private and public violence against women in the conference's Declaration and Programme of Action was a result of a global campaign involving over nine hundred women's groups worldwide. While the Vienna Declaration is not a binding treaty, it was agreed to by the 171 countries in attendance and reflects the verbal commitment of countries around the world to address violence against women as a human rights violation.

Spurred by the Vienna World Conference on Human Rights, the UN General Assembly in 1993 adopted a Declaration on the Elimination of Violence Against Women.[117] While this instrument is not legally binding on states, it does indicate recognition of violence against women as an important human rights issue and spells out areas of violence that governments should address. This document defines violence against women broadly as any act of gender-based violence that results in, or is likely to result in, physical, sexual, or psychological harm or suffering to women, including threats of such acts, coercion or arbitrary deprivation of liberty, whether occurring in public or private life.[118] Examples of gender-based violence include:

- Physical, sexual, and psychological violence occurring in the family, including battering, sexual abuse of female children in the household, dowry-related violence, marital rape, female genital mutilation, and other traditional practices harmful to women, and nonspousal violence related to exploitation.

- Physical, sexual, and psychological violence occurring within the general community, including rape, sexual abuse, sexual harassment and intimidation at work, in educational institutions and elsewhere, and trafficking in women and forced prostitution.

- Physical, sexual, and psychological violence perpetrated or condoned by the state, wherever it occurs.[119]

The 1993 declaration provided humanitarian organizations and other groups with the first internationally accepted definition of gender-based violence that could be incorporated into agency policies and programmatic work.

Another positive outcome of the success of women's human rights advocates at the 1993 World Conference on Human Rights in Vienna was the appointment by the UN Commission on Human Rights, the primary UN body overseeing the UN human rights system, of a Special Rapporteur on Violence Against Women. Radhika Coomaraswamy, a Sri Lankan lawyer, assumed this post in March 1994 with the authority to investigate the underlying causes and consequences of abuse, as well

## Understanding the Declaration on the Elimination of Violence Against Women

The declaration defines violence broadly, including threats of violence, and outlines forms of violence that occur in both the public and private spheres. It holds governments responsible for using all possible and adequate means to eliminate all acts of violence against women. It mentions two types of state responsibility: (1) responsibility for violence committed by state authorities; and (2) responsibility for violence committed by anyone to whom the state authorities do not react properly. Governments are cautioned not to be reluctant to act because of tradition, religious, and other beliefs.

The declaration also recommends that member states consider developing national plans of action to protect women from violence or put these provisions into existing plans. In doing so, states are encouraged to consult with NGOs, especially those working in the field of violence against women. Authorities are encouraged to adopt gender-sensitive training conducted by experienced women in the field of violence against women for all officials responsible for prevention, investigation, criminal procedures, and punishment of violence against women.

*Source*: Julie Mertus with Nancy Flowers and Mallika Dutt, *Local Action/Global Change: Learning About the Human Rights of Women and Girls* (New York: UNIFEM and the Center for Women's Global Leadership, 1999).

as individual cases. The office of the special rapporteur gathers information through in-country visits and review of information submitted by NGOs and UN agencies. Annual reports to the Commission on Human Rights have focused on both war and peacetime gender violence and abuse.[120] The special rapporteur's reports have also been useful for supporting asylum claims of refugee women.[121]

Another UN special rapporteur focusing on gender issues has an even more close connection to armed conflict. The UN Subcommission on the Prevention and Protection of Minorities has appointed a special rapporteur to study the Situation of Systematic Rape, Sexual Slavery and Slavery-like Practices During Armed Conflict. Linda Chavez, a member of the subcommission, submitted a preparatory document on this question in 1993,[122] and augmented it with a working paper in 1995[123] and a preliminary report in 1996.[124] In its 53rd Session in 1997, the UN Commission on Human Rights requested that all of its thematic special rapporteurs and working groups, and many of its country-specific rapporteurs, report on government accountability for gender-specific abuses.[125] Many of these bodies report specifically on conflict situations— for example, the special rapporteurs on torture, internally displaced persons, and the working group drafting an optional protocol to the Rights of the Child Convention on children in armed conflict.

The establishment of International Criminal Tribunals for the Former Yugoslavia and Rwanda in 1994 and 1995 also served to draw attention to gender-based violence. These tribunals were given jurisdiction over grave breaches of the Geneva Conventions of 1949,[126] violations of the laws or customs of war, genocide,[127] and crimes against humanity.[128] By being specifically empowered to investigate and prosecute rape as a crime against humanity, the tribunals broke new ground in recognizing war crimes against women. Trials were begun in 1995 and 1996 and included the charge of rape and other forms of sexual violence. The Tribunal Rules of Procedure and Evidence provide a series of measures designed to protect witnesses testifying before the tribunal. However, women still fear testifying before the tribunal because witness safeguards are far from perfect, protections for family members virtually nonexistent, and education of court personnel and investigators on gender issues often lacking.

One of the most significant regional developments on gender issues was the 1995 Inter-American Convention on the Prevention, Punishment and Eradication of Violence Against Women.[129] This declaration provides women victims of violence in the Americas with recourse to the existing regional mechanisms: the Inter-American Court, the Inter-American Commission on Human Rights, as well as an Inter-American Commission for Women. An earlier declaration of the Council of Europe, the 1991 Declaration on the Elimination of Sexual Violence,[130] asserted that violence against women should be regarded as a human rights violation.

The World Conference for Women in 1995 paid considerable attention to gender-based violence and to other issues facing women in conflict. The Beijing Platform for Action addressed violence against women as one of its strategic areas of concern, with specific attention to the issue of women in armed conflict. The Beijing Platform for Action implores governments to "cooperate with and assist the Special Rapporteur on Violence Against Women in the performance of her mandate and furnish all information requested."[131] This means that women can encourage and assist their governments to give information about violence against women to the special rapporteur as well as request her to investigate violations in their countries. The Women's Commission for Refugee Women and Children was one of the NGOs that took a leading role in formulating sections of the Beijing Platform for Action pertaining to armed conflict.

The Beijing Platform for Action specifically calls for international attention to the particular concerns of refugee women. It recognizes that women refugees face increased burdens in their families "as a result of conflict, unexpectedly cast as sole manager of household, sole parent, and caretaker of elder relatives."[132] It acknowledges that "[w]omen are vulnerable to gender-specific violations of human rights while fleeing, or relocating across borders, including rape and systematic rape, that is use of rape by enemy forces as a calculated campaign of terror and destruction."[133] The Beijing Platform for Action observes: "Women often experience difficulty in countries of asylum in being recognized as refugees when the claim is based on gender-related persecution."[134] Finally, it emphasizes the importance of participation in ensuring that gender-related concerns are integrated into the existing mechanisms designed to protect refugees. "The strength and resilience that women refugees display in the face of displacement is not acknowledged. Women's voices need to be represented in policymaking that affects them, including in processes to prevent conflicts before they result in the need for communities to flee."[135] The Commission on the Status of Women, a UN body that meets annually, is specifically charged with implementing the Beijing Platform for Action.

The accomplishments in Beijing extend far beyond the words of the document. Nearly every humanitarian and human rights organization that deals with women responded to the issues raised. Before the conference, Beijing was a rallying cry for change within many organizations, an opportunity for internal audits of gender policies and, at the very least, a chance to create reports for presentation in Beijing and to organize the staff who would attend. Those who attended the conference experienced an exceptional networking opportunity, meeting colleagues and adversaries and discussing every issue. A specific place to discuss refugee women's problems provided one focal point, but attendees could choose from discussions of numerous cross-cutting themes. Plans were developed for future work, programs tested, lessons learned on gender issues identified. After the conference, many aid agencies changed their policies and operations to better cope with gender problems, as elaborated in the following chapter.

As a result of developments reviewed above, gender-based violence in wartime and peacetime enjoyed a prominent place by the end of the 1990s on the international agenda as a human rights concern.

## Conclusion

International human rights, humanitarian, and refugee law as it has evolved over the centuries and particularly in the period since World War II offers a framework for policies and practices related to gender in humanitarian crises. The framework sheds light on all three levels of inquiry summarized in the Conclusion of Chapter 2. Informed by this normative framework, protection and assistance efforts by humanitarian organizations will be more sensitive to gender issues and better able to respond to such concerns justly and effectively.

Agencies should train staff in the fundamentals of the legal developments presented in this chapter and, if necessary, create the position of women's human rights advocate to integrate these concerns into policy and programming. Should their goals permit, aid agencies may consider becoming more involved in using UN human rights mechanisms and humanitarian law to enhance protection.

NGOs may submit information to the Special Rapporteur on Violence Against Women and to countries that are scheduled to present country reports to the CEDAW and CRC. The trend toward greater recognition of gender issues in international institutions creates new opportunities for advancing humanitarian goals of providing protection and assistance. Individual organizations must decide for themselves how to take advantage of these opportunities.

# LOOKING AHEAD

THIS CHAPTER IDENTIFIES current trends among humanitarian organizations responding to gender problems and suggests recommendations
for further action. It draws together innovative elements in agency policy
and practice noted in Chapters 2 and 3 and comments on the process of
institutional learning and change pertaining to gender. As with the preceding chapters, interviews with staff of NGOs, UN High Commissioner
for Refugees, the UN Office of the High Commissioner for Human Rights,
and other intergovernmental and governmental organizations form the
basis of this analysis. While written with the specific needs of humanitarian agencies in mind, the material may also be of interest to academics
and policymakers.

## Trend 1: Creation of Gender Policies and Gender Strategies

Humanitarian organizations have begun to realize that involving
women in programmatic activities is "not solely a matter of equity but,
in a range of activities, a condition for achieving development and, as
far as projects are concerned, a condition of their success also."[1] Many
humanitarian groups have taken steps to integrate gender throughout
their programming. This entails, at the initial stage, establishing a policy
on gender indicating goals and creating a gender strategy for achieving
these goals.

The policy of the Canadian International Development Agency
(CIDA) provides one innovative model. Its goals with respect to gender are

- to support the objectives and initiatives of women in developing countries;

- to achieve greater understanding of actual and potential roles for women in developing countries;

- to increase participation of women in design, implementation, and evaluation of development projects;

- to include women in CIDA programs and projects in proportion to their existing participation rates in the target groups;

- to work in partnership with recipient governments to close economic gaps between men and women in their countries;

- to emphasize strategies to assist women in income generation, including reduction of demands on their time and energy from household work and food production; and

- to support special women's programs linked to overall development where special efforts are required.[2]

Lutheran World Relief (LWR) provides another illustration of innovations in policies pertaining to gender. In 1993–94, LWR made gender equity one of its cross-cutting themes and thus a priority throughout the organization. One of its first steps was to develop a gender equity statement:

We strive to incorporate awareness, attitudes and measures which promote gender equity through all aspects of the life of Lutheran World Relief and its partners. We also strive to ensure that projects favorably impact women. Addressing the particular needs of women as well as men in their respective communities and strengthening their voices in planning and implementation enhances the impact and sustainability of development efforts.

The foregoing policy statement is supported by specific gender strategies. LWR asserts that local leadership must play a key role with LWR as an institution as well as in its relief and development efforts. The organization sees gender equity as a central issue within its own operations and it vows to examine its governance and management to identify, eliminate, and prevent gender inequality. Other strategic aims include

- focusing on advocacy, education, and management to identify, eliminate, and prevent gender inequality and bias;

- accompanying partners through exchange and training as they seek to deepen their understanding, commitment, and competence;

- engaging in dialogue with partners at the stages of planning, implementation, and evaluating projects;

- gathering and disseminating gender assessment tools, methodologies, and approaches;

- sharing particularly effective practices regarding gender equity that have been developed and applied; and

- gathering sex-specific data on the impact of projects.[3]

The attempts by LWR to create an effective gender strategy have been aided by broad staff participation. LWR has implemented its gender strategy through the development of tools at its headquarters in New York and through training and projects with offices and partner organizations in the field.[4] A central component was the development of regional gender plans to deal with integration while recognizing and respecting the variety and diversity of partners worldwide. LWR designed a Gender Packet to guide partners and field officers,[5] including a Counterpart Agency Gender Study (CAGS) as a diagnostic tool for partner organizations.[6]

The study's objectives include finding out how well LWR counterparts have integrated gender into their work, determining whether there is an interest in gender integration, assessing the conditions that can act as a catalyst or constraint, and learning how partners want LWR to help them integrate gender. Through an interactive process, carried out electronically and in face-to-face meetings, LWR field offices reached a consensus on the questions that would be asked on these CAGS objectives.[7] Catholic Relief Services has embarked on a similar process of incorporating gender into its programming by way of a strong policy statement and by soliciting staff feedback on creating and implementing gender strategies.[8]

## Recommendations

- Create a gender policy that underscores the importance of both men and women benefiting from international assistance that recognizes their different needs and improves their roles in decision-making.

- Link policy to concrete steps and timetable for implementation.

- Design mechanisms for monitoring compliance with gender policy and gender strategy.

## Trend 2: Increased Organizational Awareness of Gender and Human Rights

Emergency relief and human rights organizations have operated synergistically in creating innovations. Pressure from aid groups has leavened the loaf of broader human rights awareness. At the same time, assistance organizations have been profoundly influenced by the heightened awareness of gender problems promoted by human rights advocates.

As discussed in Chapter 3, the heightened awareness of gender violence and abuse in war and peacetime has been inspired by the global movement for women's human rights. "In attempting to unveil the female face of persecution of its victims, advocacy organizations have documented such abuses as sexual violence in all its forms."[9] Efforts of human rights advocates to expose abuses against women have had important implications for refugee, displaced, and war-imperiled women. These efforts have provided the kind of information necessary for women to make claims of gender-based persecution under the Refugee Convention. In addition, they have exposed the failures of aid organizations to offer adequate protection and assistance.

As a result, when human rights groups document and publicize abuses against women, relief agencies are called to account for the ways in which their policies and programs have responded or, more negatively, have complicated the situation. When they fail to offer a plan for protecting and assisting women, their public—the general public, donors, and, for a membership organization, their members—is now likely to demand an explanation. The widespread publicity regarding rape in Bosnia and the tremendous outpouring of sympathy for victims created intense pressure on humanitarian groups to respond, although with mixed results. Violence against women in conflicts elsewhere has not been exposed equally well. Nonetheless, the trend since the rapes in Bosnia were publicized at the end of 1992 and the World Conference on Human Rights recognized violence against women as a war crime in 1993 has been for aid organizations to be increasingly vigilant about women's human rights.

More public discussion of women's human rights has fostered greater awareness of protection and assistance problems pertaining to women. Aid organizations have become more conscious of the different needs of males and females for physical protection, legal registration, status determination, and assistance. Also, the agencies are more attuned to gender bias with respect to basic needs and human rights, and abuse that targets females.

These steps are significant. Nonetheless, aid organizations have one additional step, which is to recognize the different capabilities that women bring to working on these problems. Humanitarian organizations are only beginning to disaggregate population data so that they may identify and properly help men and women.[10]

## Recommendations

- For each assistance and protection effort in a given country, identify the different needs of males and females with respect to physical protection, legal registration, and status determination; gender bias with respect to meeting basic needs and respecting human rights; sexual or other physical violence targeting females; and the different capabilities and responsibilities that women could bring to creating and implementing protection and assistance plans.

- Conduct training sessions with management and staff on women's human rights and on the fundamentals of humanitarian law pertaining to gender, including information on gender-based violence as a human rights issue.

## Trend 3: Integration of Gender into Agency Activities

Movements to improve gender programs within agencies have generally taken one of two conflicting courses: mainstreaming of gender throughout an organization and all programs, or establishing a gender focal point or unit within an organization. The latter concept is straightforward: each organization would have at least one focal point to ensure that gender problems receive attention, and offer expertise to other parts of the organization. The mainstreaming concept, however, is more complex.

Mainstreaming began as an effort to increase the effectiveness of development programs in incorporating women and women's problems. Today, the concept is applied in the humanitarian field to refer to "achieving women's full participation with men in decisionmaking; getting women's problems centralized (not just near the center); putting women on a par with men in the process of initiating . . . activities."[11]

Both approaches have drawbacks. Mainstreaming risks submerging gender within the organization so that the problems are no longer given attention. It may also result in words on paper but few changes in programming. For example, a UN mission to Afghanistan in 1997 found that "several agencies have developed their own guidelines for gender mainstreaming, but these are rarely followed. Many agencies do not address gender concerns in the design, implementation or monitoring phases of their work . . ."[12]

But the gender focal point approach risks marginalizing gender within the organization so that it is treated as something "special" that is not to be dealt with at all apart from the activities of the specified unit. As a result, there is little guarantee that gender problems will be found in any other projects than those which are explicitly about women.

In either approach, organizations may also hold special meetings, training, and workshops on gender and establish mechanisms to report regularly on problems pertaining to gender. Often these steps are accompanied by the hiring of additional personnel. While such personnel may add more women to mid-level management, they rarely are top-level decision-makers. The upper-level management of most humanitarian organizations remains overwhelmingly male.

## Recommendations

- Establish a gender unit or focal point with the explicit role of promoting gender perspectives or, alternatively, make gender part of everyone's job, working at the same time to delimit the drawbacks of either approach.

- Assess personnel policies throughout the organization according to a gender perspective and adopt changes to meet gender concerns.

- Conduct gender training for senior management and for staff to enhance gender awareness, sensitization, analysis, planning, implementation, monitoring, and evaluation.

- Link job performance expectations and evaluations to advancement of gender policy and strategy.

## Trend 4: Programmatic Innovations Pertaining to Gender

International policy changes and efforts to mainstream gender are accompanied by specific programmatic changes. While the changes differ according to the mission, history, focus, and nature of the specific organization, the most ambitious seek to do the following:[13]

- Involve refugee, internally displaced, and war-affected women in the design and implementation of all programs dealing with them.

- Include information about refugee women, preferably by the women themselves, in all educational activities carried out in programs for war-affected women. Include information in public media campaigns to combat abuse of and discrimination against them.

- Make it a practice to deal with all incidents of sexual violence and to respond to related protection and assistance problems.

- Improve the design of refugee and displaced persons camps to promote greater security according to the needs voiced by women. Such measures could include better lighting; security patrols; placement of latrines and washing facilities; access to water, food, and wood; and special accommodations for single women, women heads of household, and unaccompanied minors.

- Offer gender-sensitive and culturally appropriate counseling to women victims. This counseling should be conducted by trained counselors, drawing from the women's culture and community.

- Support the operation of emergency hotlines and safe houses, staffed where possible by the women themselves or women counselors.

- Provide emergency resettlement to refugee women who may be particularly exposed to abuse.

- Ensure that refugee and internally displaced women are not forced to stay for long periods in closed camps or detention centers where they are more likely to be the victims of violence.

- Employ female protection officers and social workers to provide remedies for women who are victims of violence.

- Place international staff that has received gender-sensitive training in border areas which women cross to enter countries of asylum as well as in reception centers, refugee camps, and settlements.

- Ensure that all staff have copies of and have training in the implementation of the UNHCR *Guidelines for the Protection of Refugee Women* and the UNHCR's *Report on Sexual Violence Against Refugees: Guidelines on Prevention and Response.*

- Provide gender-sensitive training for host country border guards, police, military units, asylum officers, aid personnel, and others who come in contact with war-affected women.

## Recommendations

- Adopt programmatic changes to address gender problems such as all of those listed above and build in flexibility to adapt to changed circumstances.

- Establish indicators for measuring the success of programs pertaining to gender and link indicators of success to satisfaction of these measures.

- Create partnerships with local women leaders who can offer advice on programming and conduct outreach to other local women. Support the efforts of local women to organize themselves.[14]

- Audit programmatic innovations. Examine both the effectiveness in reaching intended goals and unexpected benefits or drawbacks of programs. The accompanying gender audit may be a useful tool.

## Trend 5: Supporting International Activities as Triggers for Change

World conferences have played a key role as catalysts for change. In particular, many aid organizations changed their practices in response to the 1993 World Conference on Human Rights in Vienna and the 1995 World Conference on Women in Beijing. The Vienna meeting was a watershed in prompting many humanitarian organizations to identify and address violence against women and other human rights problems.

For some organizations and programs, it was the point at which the word "woman" became a part of agency parlance. For others, it was the point at which existing programs targeting the concerns of women in conflict situations gained momentum. Some humanitarian organizations created policies, public education material, and programs for Beijing; many more revised these after Beijing.[15] Beijing was the point at which usage of the word "woman" evolved into the word "gender" in many organizational policies and programs.

Another highly significant agent reinforcing pressure from the international level has been pressure from the field. While field staff can block programs for pragmatic reasons, they can promote them as well.

## Gender Audit: Questions to Ask

### Gender Impact

- What are the different needs, interests, and capacities of men and women in the target population?

- Who are the intended beneficiaries of the project and what assumptions are being made about them? Are those assumptions well-informed? Who is being overlooked?

- Who devised the goals of the intervention? Are those goals shared equally by men and women, with the same emphasis and degree of priority? Would the intervention promote gender equality?

- Whose interests are being promoted through the intervention?

- Who is likely to gain from this intervention and who is likely to lose? Which men and which women?

### Project Preparation and Planning

- Does the organization initiating the project have a stated aim in relation to gender issues?

- How does the project affect the productive, reproductive, and/or social roles of women and men—as family members and mothers or fathers, educators, agricultural producers, income earners, or community leaders?

- What proportion of the planning team are women and are their views taken into account?

- How have women among the participants and beneficiaries of the project been consulted?

- Are training opportunities available equally to women and men, and do these opportunities take into consideration their various roles and commitments?

### Project Implementation

- How are women and men involved in the execution of the plan? Are the women involved in the governing bodies, project staff, as activists and beneficiaries?

- How does that project affect women's and men's access to, and control over, resources and benefits?

- Is there continuing attention to possible changes in the pattern of women's and men's lives?

- Have women and men in the community grown in gender awareness through their involvement in the project?

*Sources*: Swedish International Development Cooperation Agency (Sida), *Overview: Gender Equality*, 2 [citing Nalia Kabeer, *Triple Roles, Gender Roles, Social Relations: The Political Sub-Text of Gender Training* (Sussex: Institute of Development Studies, 1992]; and Christian Aid, "Towards Gender-Aware Development: Ten Questions to Ask," 1989 (available at <www.oneworld.org/aprodev/good/tenq.htm>). Although these questions were originally intended to apply to development projects, they are generally applicable to humanitarian assistance and protection activities.

Innovations in protecting refugee and displaced women in camps, for example, are often driven by pragmatic field initiatives. A resourceful aid worker in the Great Lakes Region of Africa solved the problem of males hoarding food for themselves by changing the labeling on some of the boxes of biscuits to read "women's biscuits." When a rumor spread among the men that male consumers would grow breasts, women and girls suddenly had more to eat. From then on, some aid agencies specifically targeted their food provisions, creating new kinds of female-only food.[16]

Very few organizations view the UNHCR guidelines on war-imperiled women or sexual violence as catalysts for change, stating their strong belief that the guidelines are often ignored in the field. Nonetheless, some advocacy groups, such as the Women's Commission for Refugee Women and Children, have created programs specifically to promote the UNHCR guidelines. Even so, a study by Judy Benjamin, a consultant to the Woman's Commission, found a need for even more knowledge about UNHCR Guidelines among field staff.[17]

More influential as a catalyst for change has been the emergence of strong and active professional association working groups, such as InterAction, a Washington-based network of U.S. NGOs. By coordinating responses to humanitarian crises, organizing topical workshops, sharing information through reports and other publications, and providing peer recognition of pioneering efforts, InterAction has been instrumental in fostering innovations in humanitarian responses, including gender problems.

## Recommendations

- Continue involvement in international meetings, using each as an opportunity to present positive programmatic developments and to reassess organizational weaknesses with respect to gender.

- Encourage innovations among field staff with respect to gender problems and develop mechanisms for sharing such innovations organization-wide.

- Improve knowledge of UNHCR guidelines and other international instruments by conducting training with local and expatriate staff; include refugee and displaced women in such efforts.

## Trend 6: Development of Nomenclature

Humanitarian organizations continue to debate whether to use the word "women" or "gender." The two are not interchangeable. This book has stressed the term "gender" in order to refer to the different roles that men and women play in society and thus to their different needs, interests, and capabilities. The term "woman" has more limited utility.

Some humanitarian staff view the use of the word gender as the less controversial alternative, because "saying 'women' may imply that women get more than men, but 'gender' means men and women." Staff at the International Federation of Red Cross and Red Crescent Societies (IFRC), for example, use the term "gender" instead of "woman" because gender includes both men and women while "woman" signifies treatment accorded to women and not men. In the summer of 1998, the IFRC was debating whether to add gender problems to its mandate without violating its "neutrality principle." In taking a stand against female genital mutilation, they asked, would the federation side with women or with one political group against another? As agencies take a greater advocacy role, such questions become more relevant.

By contrast, some other organizations find use of "gender" more controversial than "women." "Gender" sounds Western and radical. The International Working Group on Refugee Women, for example, steers away from use of the word gender for fear of alienating women who do not come from Western traditions.[18] Some staff voice a different concern: that in the absence of the word "women," the focus on women's human rights will be lost. To accommodate both concerns, IGOs and NGOs sometimes use both "gender" and "women." For example, a recent conference at the UN in Geneva was publicized as being about "women, conflict and gender."[19] Staff explained that the title was not redundant but simply more precise. "Women" underscored women's human rights and the notion that women's status should improve, and "gender" emphasized the different roles that men and women play in society, the different challenges they face and the different resources they bring.

### Recommendations

- Do not allow programmatic innovations to be stymied by debate over language.

- Include staff in decisions over what language to employ; encourage discussion regarding the implications of the word "gender" and "women."

- Use "woman" to emphasize that women's human rights should improve and "gender" to focus on the different needs and capacities of men and women.

## Trend 7: Tensions between Agency Policies and Operational Constraints

Agency policies on gender often are not consistent with realities in the field. Frequently, policy statements by humanitarian organizations conflict with actions taken. However, with respect to gender, particular problems exacerbate the degree of inconsistency.

At a given agency headquarters, a concrete and realistic plan of action may not exist for implementation of gender policies. Organizational decision-makers may in fact be unaware of the extent of dissonance between their policy statements on gender and operational reality. Thus, they may not even attempt to improve implementation. Many efforts undertaken to strengthen programs in relation to gender tend to focus on training in the abstract with little connection to field realities. Field staff often are not given an opportunity to reflect on their own experiences and to exchange ideas about best practices. These problems are exacerbated when women are not represented at top levels of management and decision-making.

At the office level, responses to gender problems tend to be pragmatic. Some of the most effective responses are created by staff who, as individuals, feel particularly strongly about gender problems that may not be represented as agency policy. Again, these experiences are rarely collected and shared, providing little opportunity for institutional learning. Local staff develop their own methods to deal with what appears to be cultural dissonance. If locals are disturbed by the ways a project addresses gender problems—for example, because the project challenges traditional notions about women's roles—field staff tend to handle the discomfort quietly, without addressing the difficult underlying issues. These difficulties sharpen when local women are not included among field staff or are present only as tokens. "NGOs too often hire male national staff who rely almost exclusively on other men for input and guidance from the local community."[20] Local women leaders should be consulted as well on how cultural practices should be interpreted. The lack of awareness of UNHCR guidelines and of women's human rights further aggravates the problem.

## Recommendations

- Monitor fieldwork for inconsistencies with gender policies and strategies on an ongoing basis and develop mechanisms to improve implementation.

- Include local women in field offices and give them positions of authority. Consult them when questions arise as to cultural sensitivity.

- Do not sweep difficult problems under the rug. When local people are disturbed by a project, deal with the problem in as visible and open a manner as possible.

- Train all staff in UNHCR guidelines and women's human rights and provide opportunities for staff to connect the information presented to realities in the field.

## Trend 8: Increasing Advocacy Activities

Humanitarian organizations have become increasingly involved in advocacy on gender problems. For some, this reflects a general increase in humanitarian advocacy. Others have deliberately devoted greater attention to advocacy related to women.

Three strategies characterize forays into advocacy activities concerning gender. The first stresses general humanitarian principles and underscores the long-standing mandate of the particular organization, relating both to gender problems. Nearly all humanitarian organizations that do any advocacy on gender problems take as an initial step some kind of internal advocacy: that is, an educational effort to explain to their own staff, board of directors, and constituents why their mandate covers gender. This entails relating gender to their traditional goals as an organization.

The second strategy links gender to the less-controversial problems traditionally confronting aid organizations such as health and freedom from violence. It is in the context of these problems that gender is discussed. Advocacy around female genital mutilation (FGM) thus discusses the health concerns of girls and forced mutilation as child abuse instead of raising the more controversial argument that FGM also perpetuates the subordinate status of girls and women in society. In these campaigns, "women's human rights" or "equality for women" are rarely articulated but instead presented as "human dignity" or health concerns. This approach is viewed as consistent with the principal mandate of aid agencies of promoting human welfare.

The third strategy directly addresses the cultural relativism debate. Advocacy here may stress the existence of international conventions applying to women and the consensus achieved at recent international meetings as indicators of an emergency global consensus on women's human rights. It may also stress that cultures are not static, pointing to voices for change within such cultures themselves. Local women's organizations are particularly helpful in developing such campaigns, which often promote alliances between aid groups and human rights agencies.

## Recommendations

- Discuss how the organization's mandate supports advocacy on gender problems; adopt policy changes, if necessary, to encourage effective advocacy on gender problems.

- Consider increased use in advocacy of international and regional human rights mechanisms, such as the submission of NGO reports to the Women's Convention and the Children's Convention and increased cooperation with the Special Rapporteur on Violence Against Women.

* Train relevant staff in advocacy techniques. Include information on the cultural relativism debate and, if relevant, on creating advocacy strategies regarding specific UN bodies.

# AFTERWORD

WOMEN ARE ORGANIZED as never before to address their human rights concerns in all aspects of life. Advocacy groups of and for women survivors of conflict are pressing to ensure that women's and men's experiences comprise an integral dimension in creating humanitarian policies and programs in which women and men benefit equally and inequalities in power relations are not perpetuated. This gender perspective has gained ground among humanitarian organizations, which now include more and more women in central decision-making roles.

Yet change does not come easily. The very design of most agencies, which are decentralized operations with fairly autonomous actors, works against top-down change. Staff members are often resistant to taking on new issues, especially in emergencies, and gender is frequently dismissed as Western and of lesser priority. As with any new directions for policies and programming, attempts to integrate gender are bound to result in missed opportunities and even unintended detrimental results. The challenge is for organizations to learn from their mistakes.

With personality-driven programs and frequent staff changes, institutional learning often simply does not happen. Some organizations have engaged in conscious attempts to learn from their mistakes and to develop tools for gender programming so that staff members do not continually reinvent the wheel. Agencies are also increasingly aware that they must listen to the needs of local populations and include both local women and men in the design of projects. The results in terms of inclusiveness have been uneven, however, and systematic feedback of gender programming has been, at best, inconsistent. Agencies continue to repeat the same mistakes even as they stumble ahead.

Meanwhile, war continues its offensive on women, systematically targeting women for rape and other sexual abuse, destroying family structures, and rendering women and children particularly vulnerable to food shortages and lack of medical care. Refusing to play the role of victims, women, supported by international humanitarian and human rights law and international advocacy networks, organize for wartime survival and peacetime reconstruction. As the examples of Bosnia and Kosovo illustrate, advocates are continually adapting and applying lessons learned from the experiences of others to their own conflicts. As the experience in Afghanistan suggests, advocates are continuing to challenge humanitarian organizations to craft creative approaches to fighting discrimination against women in the name of culture.

Whenever women gain influence in humanitarian activities, the net result is, at a minimum, a favorable adjustment in the power relations between men and women and an incremental advancement of equality, at least in the short term. The ongoing challenge rests in sustaining the newer and more equitable power relations after the conflicts and postwar reconstruction efforts cease.

We find grounds for optimism in this continuing struggle. While war's offensive on women is unlikely to end in the foreseeable future, women and those committed to protect and assist them are unlikely to curtail their offensive on war. Indeed, they are using existing frameworks and creating new tools to address their plight and to improve the prospects for generations to come. These common efforts deserve support and success.

# NOTES

## Chapter 1

1. United Nations Commission on the Status of Women, Report of the Secretary-General, *Peace: Refugee and Displaced Women and Children,* UN Doc. E/CN.6/1991/4, Vienna (November 9, 1990).
2. EUROSTEP, *Gender and Humanitarian Assistance: A Eurostep Paper,* <www.oneworld.org/eurostep.gender.htm> (May 22, 1996) [hereafter *Eurostep Paper*].
3. Francis Deng and Roberta Cohen, *Masses in Flight: The Global Crisis of Internal Displacement* (Washington, D.C.: The Brookings Institution, 1998).
4. This definition of gender is found in United Nations Commission on Human Rights, Report of the Secretary-General, *Integrating the Human Rights of Women Throughout the United Nations System,* UN Doc. E/CN.4/1997/40, (December 20, 1996) [hereafter "Integrating Women"].
5. This paper does not settle the question of what constitutes human rights and what are human needs. Certainly, human rights reflect human needs. Under traditional international law, not all human needs (for example, the need for a feeling of security or for love) are themselves human rights.
6. Beth Woroniuk, et al., *Overview: Gender Equality and Emergency Assistance/Conflict Resolution* (Stockholm: Swedish International Development Cooperation Agency, January 1997), 1.
7. Roberta Cohen, *Refugee and Internally Displaced Women: A Development Perspective* (Washington D.C.: The Brookings Institution, 1995).
8. See Human Rights Watch (Africa Watch and Women's Rights Project), *Seeking Refuge, Finding Terror: The Widespread Rape of Somali Women Refugees in North Eastern Kenya,* Human Rights Watch Short Report 5, no. 13 (October 1993) and Human Rights Watch (Women's Rights Project), *Human Rights Watch: Global Report on Women's Human Rights* (New York: Human Rights Watch, 1995), 100–139, 120.
9. America's Watch and Women's Rights Project, *Untold Terror: Violence Against Women in Peru's Armed Conflict* (New York: Human Rights Watch, 1992).
10. Human Rights Watch (Africa Watch and Women's Rights Project), *Shat-*

*tered Lives: Sexual Violence During the Rwandan Genocide and its Aftermath* (New York: Human Rights Watch, 1996).

11. Judy El-Bushra and Cecile Mukarubuga, "Women, War and Transition," *Gender and Development* 3, no. 3 (1995), 16–22.

12. Eshila Maravanyika, *Some Issues of Protection and Participation of Refugee Women: The Case of Mozambican Refugee Women in Zimbabwean Camps* (The Hague: Institute of Social Studies, July 1995).

13. See, for example, Anne M. Gomez, "The New INS Guidelines on Gender Persecution: Their Effect on Asylum in the United States for Women Fleeing the Forced Sterilization and Abortion Policies of the People's Republic of China," *North Carolina Journal of International Law and Commercial Regulation* 21 (1996), 621.

14. See Human Rights Watch, *Global Report on Women's Human Rights* (New York: Human Rights Watch, 1995).

15. Author's interviews in Pristina, July 1998.

16. See Emily Love, "Equality in Political Asylum Law: For a Legislative Recognition of Gender-Based Persecution," *Harvard Women's Law Journal* no. 17 (1994), 133. For an unsuccessful asylum claim in this regard, see Khaefyazdani v. INS, No. 93-9514, 1993 U.S. App. LEXIS 21716 (10th Cir. Aug. 25, 1993) (denying asylum to an Iranian woman who had been subject to police harassment for her refusal to wear traditional Muslim attire on the basis that "harassment was typical of that experienced by all women in a closed, totalitarian society").

17. Jodi Jacobsen, *Environmental Refugees: A Yardstick for Humanity*, Worldwatch Paper No. 86 (Washington, D.C.: Worldwatch Institute, 1988).

18. For a discussion of refugees as products of underdevelopment, see Charles P. Keely, *Global Refugee Policy: The Case for a Development-Oriented Strategy* (New York: Population Council, 1981).

19. Suzanne Schmeidl, "Comparative Trends in Forced Displacement: IDPs and Refugees, 1964–96," in Norwegian Refugee Council, *Internally Displaced People: A Global Survey* (London: Earthscan Publications, Ltd., 1999).

20. Elizabeth E. Ruddick, "The Continuing Constraint of Sovereignty: International Law, International Protection, and the Internally Displaced," *Boston University Law Review* no. 77 (1997), 429. See also Deng and Cohen, *Masses in Flight*.

21. Cohen, *Refugee and Internally Displaced Women*, 1.

22. See Judy A. Benjamin and Khadija Fancy, *The Gender Dimensions of Internal Displacement: Concept Paper and Annotated Bibliography*, Submitted to the Office of Emergency Programmes, UNICEF, for the Women's Commission for Refugee Women and Children, September 1998.

23. Benjamin and Fancy, *The Gender Dimensions of Internal Displacement*, 10.

24. Benjamin and Fancy, *The Gender Dimensions of Internal Displacement*, 10.

25. See Judith Gail Gardham, *Non-Combatant Immunity as a Norm of International Humanitarian Law* (Dordrecht: Martinus Nijhoff, 1993);

and Richard Shelly Hartigan, *The Forgotten Victim: A History of the Civilian* (Chicago: Precedent Publishing, 1982).

26. Beijing Platform for Action, para. 113.

27. Patricia Tuitt, *False Images: Law's Construction of Refugee Status* (London: Pluto Press, 1996), 33–34.

28. Teresa L. Peters, "International Refugee Law and the Treatment of Gender-Based Persecution: International Initiatives as a Model and Mandate for National Reform," *Transnational Law and Contemporary Problems* 6 (1996), 225.

29. United Nations High Commission for Refugees, *Guidelines for the Protection of Refugee Women*, UN Doc. ES/SCP/67 (1991), 32–35. See also Lauren Gilbert, "Rights, Refugee Women and Reproductive Health," *American University Law Review* no. 44 (1995), 1213.

30. *Eurostep Paper*, para. 3.31.

31. See Kelly Dawn Askin, *War Crimes Against Women: Prosecution in International Tribunals* (The Hague: Martinus Nijhoff Publishers, 1997); Susan Brownmiller, *Against Our Will: Men, Women and Rape* (London: Secker & Warburg, 1975); Adrien Katherine Wrong and Sylke Merchan, "Rape, Ethnicity and Culture: Spirit Injury from Bosnia to Black America," *Columbia Human Rights Law Review* no. 25 (1995), 1; and Peter Karsten, *Soldiers and Combat* (Westport, Conn.: Greenwood Press, 1978).

32. See Commission on Human Rights, *Report of the Special Rapporteur on Violence Against Women*, UN Doc. E/CN.4/1998/54/Add.1, 4 (February 1998); Deborah E. Anker, "Women Refugees: Forgotten No Longer?," *San Diego Law Review* 32 (1995), 771, 787 (excerpted from the Inter-American Commission on Human Rights, Organization of American States, *Report of the Situation on Human Rights*); Amnesty International, *Bosnia-Herzegovina: Rape and Sexual Abuse by Armed Forces*, Doc. EUR. 63/01/93 (1993); Commission on Human Rights, Report of the Secretary-General, *Rape and Abuse of Women in the Territory of the Former Yugoslavia*, UN Doc. E/CN.4/1995/4 (June 13, 1993); and Anne-Marie O'Connor, "Politically Motivated Rape Common Weapon in Haiti," *Palm Beach Post*, Jan. 9, 1994, 1A.

33. Ruth Seifert, *War and Rape: Analytical Approaches* (Geneva: Women's International League for Peace and Freedom, 1993), 1.

34. Seifert, *War and Rape*, 1.

35. Susan Brownmiller, "Making Female Bodies the Battlefield," in Alexandra Stiglmayer, ed., *Mass Rape: The War Against Women in Bosnia-Herzegovina* (Lincoln: University of Nebraska Press, 1994), 38.

36. See Julie Mertus, "Women in the Service of National Identity," *Hastings Women's Law Journal* 5, no. 1 (1994), 5.

37. Brownmiller, "Making Female Bodies the Battlefield," 181.

38. Brownmiller, *Against Our Will*, 107. See also Madeline Morris, "By Force of Arms: Rape, War, and Military Culture," *Duke Law Journal* 45 (1996), 651.

39. See C. E. J. de Nef and S. J. de Ruiter, *Sexual Violence Against Women Refugees* (The Hague: Ministry for Social Affairs, 1984).

40. See, for example, Julie Mertus, *Internal Displacement in Kosovo: The*

*Impact on Women and Children: A Field Report Assessing the Emergency and Making Recommendations on an Effective Humanitarian Response* (New York: Women's Commission for Refugee Women and Children, June 1998).

41. Judy El-Bushra and Eugenia Pia Lopes, "The Gender of Armed Conflict," in *Development and Conflict: The Gender Dimension* (Oxford: Oxfam, 1994), 18–28.

42. M. Casey, "Domestic Violence Against Women: The Women's Perspective," in Charlotte Bunch and Niamh Reilly, *Demanding Accountability: The Global Campaign and Vienna Tribune for Women's Rights* (New Jersey: Center for Women's Global Leadership and UNIFEM, 1994).

43. For examples, see generally, Susan Forbes Martin, *Refugee Women* (London: Zed Books, 1992).

44. Amnesty International, *Human Rights Are Women's Rights* (London: Amnesty International, 1995), 25–26; and Human Rights Watch, *Human Rights Watch Global Report on Women's Human Rights* (New York: Human Rights Watch, 1995), 183.

45. Mertus, Julie, et al., *The Suitcase: Refugee Voices from Bosnia and Croatia* (Berkeley: University of California Press, 1997).

46. Marin, Leni and Blandina Lansang-de Mesa, eds., *Women on the Move: Proceedings of Workshop on Human Rights Abuses Against Immigrant & Refugee Women* (London: Family Violence Prevention Fund, 1993), 12.

47. B.a.B.e., *Status of Women's Rights in Croatia* (Zagreb: B.a.B.e., 1994), 2.

48. Julie Mertus and Rachel Pine, *Meeting the Health Care Needs of Women Survivors of the Balkan Conflict* (New York: The Centre for Reproductive Law and Policy, 1993).

49. Many of the humanitarian groups interviewed for this report noted an improvement with respect to the provision of humanitarian aid packages, yet at the same time they indicated the need for further sensitivity to the needs and concerns of women and girls.

50. Pippa Scott and May Anne Schwalbe, *A Living Wall: Former Yugoslavia: Zagreb, Slavonski Brod & Sarajevo, October 3–18, 1993* (New York: Women's Commission for Refugee Women and Children, 1993), 8.

51. UNIFEM, *Integration of Women's Human Rights into the Work of the Special Rapporteurs*, Report for the 53rd Session of the Commission on Human Rights Agenda Item 9(a), "Further Promotion and Encouragement of Human Rights and Fundamental Freedoms, Including the Question of the Programme and Methods of Work of the Commission, Alternative Approaches and Ways and Means within the United Nations System for Improving the Effective Enjoyment of Human Rights and Fundamental Freedoms," UN Doc. E/CN.4/1997/131.

52. UNHCR Policy on Refugee Women, 1990, 6.

53. *Integrating Women* at 5, para. 10.

54. Teresa Hanley, *Dealing with Diversity: Gender in Disaster-Related Work of the Federation* (London: British Red Cross, August 1997) [hereafter *Dealing with Diversity*, at Glossary].

55. *Report of the 1995 UN Expert Group Meeting on the Development of Guidelines for the Integration of Gender Perspectives in UN Human*

*Rights Activities and Programmes*, E/CN.4/1996/105.

56. Hanley, *Dealing with Diversity*, Glossary.

57. This definition is taken from the Glossary in Julie Mertus with Nancy Flowers and Mallika Dutt, *Local Action/Global Change: Learning About the Human Rights of Women and Girls* (New York: UNIFEM and the Center for Women's Global Leadership, 1999). See this glossary for other gender-related terms.

58. B. Byrne and S. Baden, *Gender, Emergencies and Humanitarian Assistance* (WID, European Commission, 1995), 9.

59. *Integrating Women* at 5, para. 10.

60. *Integrating Women* at 5, para. 10.

61. Mertus, Flowers and Dutt, *Local Action/Global Change*, p. 241.

62. UN Declaration on Violence Against Women.

63. Mertus, Flowers and Dutt, *Local Action/Global Change*, p. 241.

## Chapter 2

1. J. Samuel Barkin and Bruce Cronin, "The State and the Nation: Changing Norms and Rules of Sovereignty in International Relations," *International Organizations* 48 (1994), 130. See also Mark Frohardt, Diane Paul and Larry Minear, *Protecting Human Rights: The Challenge to Humanitarian Organizations*, Occasional Paper #35 (Providence, R.I.: Watson Institute, 1999), chap. 1.

2. See, for example, Helsinki Watch, *War Crimes in Bosnia-Hercegovina 2* (New York: Human Rights Watch, 1993).

3. For a critique of open-city models to protect minority populations, see International Crisis Group, *The Konjic Conundrum: Why Minorities Have Failed to Return to Model Open City* (Sarajevo: International Crisis Group, 1988). See also International Crisis Group, *Minority Return or Mass Relocation?* (Sarajevo: International Crisis Group, 1998). It is interesting to note that one of the problems associated with the failure of the UNHCR open-city initiative in Vogosca is that the municipality currently hosts over seven thousand displaced Bosnians, most of whom are women. They are opposed to minority returns because they currently live in homes of displaced persons and fear they will be forced out upon the return of minorities. Their presence made Vogosca unsuitable as an open city without attention to their needs. Helsinki Watch, *War Crimes*, 17.

4. Roland Salvisberg, Office of the High Commissioner, Sarajevo, June 1998 (paraphrasing Paul Stubbs).

5. International Council of Voluntary Agencies, Sarajevo, June 1998.

6. This section draws from the author's work in the field from 1993–95, and interviews conducted in Bosnia in 1988.

7. In 1994–95, the author conducted numerous interviews with refugees, displaced persons, and war-imperiled populations where such complaints were widespread. In 1998, the author spoke with women who survived the war in Sarajevo, Tuzla, and Mostar; they told similar stories about outdated medicines and inappropriate supplies. See also Jan Goodwin, "A Nation of Widows," *On the Issues* (Spring 1997), 28, 31.

8. Stories abound about humanitarian field workers who undertook to safeguard a particular family, for example by moving into their home and living with them, or by bribing UNPROFOR troops for safe passage for the family.

9. "Raped women" is in quotation marks because this is the language that many outsiders would use in seeking such women. Local women experienced such phraseology as demeaning because it reduces all women who have experienced rape to that one attribute: they become defined by the rape alone and all other aspects of their existence are discounted.

10. Belgrade and Geneva IOM offices, interviews conducted in 1994 and 1995.

11. Belgrade and Geneva IOM offices, interviews conducted in 1994 and 1995.

12. Mme. B. L. Bayarmaa, Head, Women and Development Unit, International Federation of the Red Cross and Red Crescent Societies, Geneva, June 1998. Much of the move to "developmental relief" came during the Cold War when people lived in refugee camps for extended periods of time.

13. Sabina Frasier and Mariana Rukovina, Democratization Program, Organization for Security and Cooperation in Europe, Sarajevo, June 1998.

14. Interview, Tuzla, 1998.

15. Ian Smillie, *Service Delivery or Civil Society? Non-Governmental Organizations in Bosnia and Herzegovina* (Ottawa: Care Canada, 1996).

16. Monika Kleck and Gordana Djuric, Prijateljice/Amica, Tuzla, July 1998.

17. Mary Hunt, IRC Tuzla, July 1998.

18. Duska Andric-Ruzick and Rada Stakic-Domuz, Medica Zenica, June 1998.

19. Elmida Saric, Zene za Zene u Bosni (Women for Women in Bosnia), Sarajevo, June 1998.

20. Julia Gerte, OSCE, Mostar, July 1998.

21. The author heard these words repeatedly during her travels in Bosnia. See also Goodwin, "A Nation of Widows," note 8 at 31.

22. Smillie, *Service Delivery or Civil Society?*, note 16.

23. Fahira Custovic (lawyer) and Azra Hasanbegovic (director), Zena BiH, Mostar, July 1998. Still, for some reason the Bosnian Women's Initiative has passed them by, perhaps because fewer of their members speak English or German than other groups and because they are less slick than some other groups.

24. See Liz Roman Gallese, "Bosnian Women Knit Their Nation Back Together," *Boston Globe*, April 12, 1998, D1.

25. Interview in Sarajevo, June 1998.

26. Others include the World Bank, the European Community Humanitarian Office (ECHO), and the EC PHARE Programme.

27. Goodwin, "A Nation of Widows," note 8 at 29.

28. Bosnian Women's Initiative, *Information Paper No. 12*, May 12, 1998, UNHCR, Office of the Chief of Mission, Bosnia and Herzegovina.

29. Interview with Homayra Etemadi, coordinator of The International Working Group on Refugee Women, formerly of the Catholic Migration Commission, Geneva, June 1998.

30. Nurdzihana Dozic, Zena 21, Sarajevo, June 1998.

31. Bosnian Women's Initiative, *Information Paper No. 12*, 2.

32. Smillie, *Service Delivery or Civil Society?*, iii.

33. This point was made by Mediha Filipvic, the only woman elected to parliament in the first Bosnian elections. Interview in Sarajevo, July 1998.

34. Jadranka Milicevic, Zene Zenama, Sarajevo, June 1998.

35. Julia Gerte, OSCE, Mostar, July 1998.

36. This section is adapted from Julie Mertus, *Internal Displacement in Kosovo: The Impact on Women and Children: A Field Report Assessing the Emergency and Making Recommendations on an Effective Humanitarian Response* (New York: Women's Commission for Refugee Women and Children, June 1998).

37. Larry Minear, Ted van Baarda and Marc Sommers, *NATO and Humanitarian Action in the Kosovo Crisis*, Occasional Paper # 36 (Providence, R.I.: Watson Institute, 2000), chap. 9.

38. See Human Rights Watch, *Humanitarian Law Violations in Kosovo* (October 1998), <http://www.hrw.org/hrw/reports98/kosovo/>. See also Physicians for Human Rights, *Medical Group Recounts Individual Testimonies of Human Rights Abuses in Kosovo* (June 24, 1998), <http://www.phrusa.org/research/kosovo2.html>; Physicians for Human Rights, *Action Alert: Kosovo Crisis* (August 1998), <http://www.phrusa.org/campaigns/kosovo.html#INVESTI>.

39. This is the estimate of the UN Office for the Coordination of Humanitarian Affairs (OCHA). See Relief Web, Revision of the 1999 United Nations Consolidated InterAgency Appeal for the Southeastern Europe Humanitarian Operation, July 26, 1999, <http://www.reliefweb.int> [hereafter "OCHA Report"]. For a chronology of major events during the period January 1, 1998–July 1999, see Minear, van Baarda, and Sommers, *NATO and Humanitarian Action*, chap. 9.

40. This section deals mainly with assistance activities, which predominate at the time of writing.

41. The results of the survey are consistent with anecdotal evidence collected by the author.

42. Resolution 1203 (1998), adopted by the Security Council at its 3937th meeting, on October 24, 1998, <http://www.nato.int/kosovo/docu/u981024a.htm>.

43. Human Rights Watch, *Detention and Abuse in Kosovo* (December 1998), <http://www.hrw.org/hrw/reports98/kosovo2/>.

44. Human Rights Watch, *Yugoslav Government War Crimes in Racak* (January 1999), <http://www.hrw.org/hrw/campaigns/kosovo98/racak.htm>; Human Rights Watch, *Human Rights Watch Investigation Finds: Yugoslav Forces Guilty of War Crimes in Racak*, Kosovo (January 29, 1999), <http://www.hrw.org/hrw/press/1999/apr/kosovo402.htm>. See also Human Rights Watch, *A Week of Terror in Drenica* (February 1999), <http://www.hrw.org/hrw/reports/1999/kosovo/>.

45. UNHCR, *Concept Paper on a Proposed Framework for Return of Refugees and Internally Displaced Persons to Kosovo* (May 12, 1999).

46. Information drawn from author's interviews with refugees in Albania, May 1999.

47. Resolution 1244 (1999), adopted by the Security Council, on June 10, 1999. The full text of the UN Resolution on Kosovo can be found at <http://www.nato.int/kosovo/docu/u990610a.htm>.

48. Kosovo Crisis Fact Sheet #110, <http://www.reliefweb.int>.

49. Kosovo Crisis Fact Sheet #110.

50. UNHCR Refugees Daily (December 10, 1999), <http://www.unhcr.ch/refworld/cgibin/newscountry.pl?country=Federal%20Republic%20of%20 Yugoslavia&country2=Yugoslav>.

51. John Kifner, "Inquiry Estimates Serb Drive Killed 10,000 in Kosovo," The New York Times, July 18, 1999, A1.

52. OCHA Report, note 6.

53. OCHA Report.

54. See generally Julie Mertus, Kosovo: How Myths and Truths Started a War (Berkeley and London: University of California Press, 1999).

55. UNHCR, Refugees Daily (November 19, 1999), <http://www.unhcr.ch/refworld/cgi-bin/newscountry.pl?country=Federal%20Republic%20 of%20 Yugoslavia&country2=Yugoslav>.

56. See UNHCR, Kosovo Winterization Report no. 7 (December 15, 1999). <http://www.unhcr.ch/news/media/kosovo/latest.htm>.

57. The situation recalls an observation regarding the tendency of Western feminist theory to focus on gender oppression linked to intergender differences while ignoring overarching issues such as race, class, and ethnicity. See Martha Walsh, "Where Feminist Theory Failed to Meet Development Practice—A Missed Opportunity in Bosnia and Herzegovina," The European Journal of Women's Studies 5 (London: Sage Publications, 1998), 329–43.

58. Recorded in a survey by the International Committee of the Red Cross, Kabul, January 1997.

59. Burqa refers to a cloak-like pleated garment that covers the body from head to foot, fitting closely over the head and face with a mesh area in front of the eyes.

60. See Judith A. Mayotte, Disposable People? The Plight of Refugees (Maryknoll, N.Y.: Orbis Books, 1992); Barnett R. Rubin, The Fragmentation of Afghanistan: State Formation and Collapse in the International System (New Haven, Conn.: Yale University Press, 1995) and Peter Marsden, The Taliban: War, Religion and the New Order in Afghanistan (London: Zed Books, Ltd., 1999).

61. Mujahidin is the name adopted by the followers of the popular resistance movement whose objective was to rid Afghanistan of the Soviets and end communist influence. See Ralph H. Magnus and Eden Naby, Afghanistan: Mullah, Marx, and Mujahid (Boulder, Colo.: Westview Press, 1998), 135–36.

62. For in-depth treatment of the formation of the warring factions see Rubin, The Fragmentation of Afghanistan.

63. For an extensive review of the formation of the Taliban, see Marsden, The Taliban.

64. Amnesty International, Women in Afghanistan: Pawns in Men's Power Struggles, AI Index: ASA (November 11, 1999).

65. William Maley, "Women and Public Policy in Afghanistan: A Comment,"

*World Development* 24, no. 1 (1996), 203–6.

66. Sima Wali, et al., "The Impact of Political Conflict on Women: The Case of Afghanistan," *American Journal of Public Health* 89, no. 10 (October 1999).

67. Based on interviews by the author with women in Ghazni and Kabul and interviews with international health workers in Kabul in 1998 and 1999.

68. Nancy Hatch Dupree, "Afghan Women Under the Taliban," in *Fundamentalism Reborn? Afghanistan and the Taliban* (London: Hurst & Company, 1998).

69. See *Afghanistan: The Forgotten War: Human Rights Abuses and Violations of the Laws of War Since the Soviet Withdrawal*, [Asia Watch Report] (February 1991). Also see Rubin, *The Fragmentation of Afghanistan.*

70. See, for example, Diana Cammack, "Gender Relief and Politics During the Afghan War" in *Engendering Forced Migration Theory and Practice,* ed. Doreen Indra, *Refugee and Forced Migration Studies* 5 (New York: Berghahn Books, 1999).

71. UNICEF, *State of the World's Children Report* (New York and Geneva: UNICEF, 1997).

72. For further discussion, see Karen Kenny, *When Needs Are Rights: An Overview of UN Efforts to Integrate Human Rights in Humanitarian Action* (Providence, R.I.: Watson Institute, 2000).

73. See Jonathan Bartsch's report, "Afghanistan Case Study: Violent Conflict and Human Rights: A Study of Principled Decision Making in Afghanistan," CARE Internal Report (October 1998).

74. For a discussion of this and other Taliban policies that tested the approaches and resolve of international agencies, see Michael Keating, "Dilemmas of Humanitarian Assistance in Afghanistan," in *Fundamentalism Reborn?*

75. The Women's Commission for Refugee Women and Children, formed in 1989, advocates worldwide for the rights of war-affected and displaced women and children.

76. *Report of the United Nations InterAgency Gender Mission to Afghanistan*, UN office of the Special Adviser on Gender Issues and Advancement of Women, New York (November 12–24, 1997).

77. See Human Rights Watch/Africa, *Shattered Lives: Sexual Violence During the Rwandan Genocide and Its Aftermath* (New York: Human Rights Watch, 1996).

78. Swedish International Development Cooperation Agency (Sida), *Overview: Gender Equality and Emergency Assistance/Conflict Resolution* (Stockholm: Sida, 1997), 1.

79. Sida, *Overview,* 2.

## Chapter 3

1. Dinah Shelton, "Private Violence, Public Wrongs, and the Responsibility of States," *Fordham International Law Journal* 13 (1989–90), 1.

2. However, for a persuasive argument that states have responsibility to

punish "private" violations of women's rights, see Rebecca J. Cook, "State Responsibility for Violations of Women's Human Rights," *Harvard Human Rights Journal* 7 (1994), 125.

3. See Charlotte Bunch, "Women's Rights as Human Rights: Toward a Revision of Human Rights," *Human Rights Quarterly* 12 (1990), 486; Hilary Charlesworth, et al., "Feminist Approaches to International Law," *American Journal of International Law* 85 (1991), 613.

4. See UN, Division for the Advancement of Women (DAW), "Sexual Violence and Armed Conflict: United Nations Responses," *Women 2000* (April 1998) [hereafter *DAW Report*]. Outlining developments pertaining to treatment of gender under international humanitarian law. For a discussion of some of the deficiencies of the application of human rights and humanitarian law to gender-based claims, see Linda A. Malone, "Beyond Bosnia and In Re Kasinga: A Feminist Perspective on Recent Developments in Protecting Women from Sexual Violence," *Boston University International Law Journal* 14 (1996), 319; and Elizabeth Adjin-Tettey, "Failure of State Protection Within the Context of the Convention Refugee Regime with Particular Reference to Gender-Related Persecution," *Journal of International Legal Studies* 3 (1997), 53.

5. Executive Committee Conclusion No. 64 (XLI), fourth preambular paragraph, and General Assembly Resolution 45/140 (1990), para. 6.

6. Kelly Dawn Askin, *War Crimes Against Women: Prosecution in International War Crimes Tribunals* (The Hague: Martinus Nijhoff Publishers, 1997), 19.

7. For example, see S. V. Viswanatha, *International Law in Ancient India* (Bombay: Longmans Green, 1925), 108–20; Emmanuel Bello, *African Customary Humanitarian Law* (London: Oyez; and Geneva: International Committee of the Red Cross, 1980), 1–62; and Majid Khadduri, *War and Peace in the Law of Islam* (Baltimore, Md.: Johns Hopkins University Press, 1955), 83–137.

8. See generally Donald A. Wells, *War Crimes and Laws of War*, 2nd ed. (Lanham, Md.: University Press of America, 1991); and Cherif M. Bassiouni, *A Draft International Criminal Code* (The Hague: Sijthoff & Noordhof, 1980), 4.

9. See generally Peter Karsten, *Soldiers and Combat* (Westport, Conn.: Greenwood Press, 1978).

10. Susan Brownmiller, *Against Our Will: Men, Women and Rape* (London: Secker & Warburg, 1975), 33.

11. Theodor Meron, *Henry's Wars and Shakespeare's Laws* (Oxford: Clarendon Press, 1993), 111–13.

12. See Geoffrey Best, *Humanity in Warfare: The Modern History of the International Law of Armed Conflicts* (London: Weidenfeld & Nicholson, 1980), 8–16. See also Maurice Keen, *The Laws of War in the Late Middle Ages* (London: Routledge and Kegan Paul, 1965).

13. Askin, *War Crimes Against Women*, 25.

14. Richard Shelly Hartigan, *The Forgotten Victim: A History of the Civilian* (Chicago: Precedent Publishing, 1965), 21.

15. Brownmiller, *Against Our Will*, 21.

16. Hartigan, *The Forgotten Victim*, 155.

17. Hugo Grotius, *De Jure Belli ac Pacis Libri Tres 2*, trans. Francis W. Kelsey (New York: Oceana Press, 1995), 656–57.

18. Brownmiller, *Against Our Will*, 35.

19. Jean-Jacques Rousseau, *On the Social Contract, Book I*, trans. Judith R. Masters (New York: St. Martin's Press, 1978), 51.

20. Askin, *War Crimes Against Women*, 28.

21. For more discussion on antecedent provisions relating to sexual violence against women in armed conflict, see Yougindra Khushalani, *Dignity and Honour of Women and Basic and Fundamental Human Rights* (The Hague and Boston: Martinus Nijhoff Publishers, 1982), 3–8.

22. For a summary of the early international process of codifying and developing the laws of war and texts of the early treaties and declarations, see Adam Roberts and Richard Guelff, eds., *Documents on the Laws of War*, 2nd ed. (Oxford: Clarendon Press, 1989).

23. 1907 Hague Convention IV Respecting the Laws and Customs of War on Land, Annex, ch. 2.

24. I. P. Trainin, "Questions of Guerrilla Warfare in the Law of War," *American Journal of International Law* 40 (1946), 354, 356 n. 2.

25. These incidents are detailed in Askin, *War Crimes Against Women*, 52–95.

26. See Askin, *War Crimes Against Women*, 88–92.

27. See generally, Peter Duus, et al., eds., *The Japanese Wartime Empire 1931–1945* (Princeton, N.J.: Princeton University Press, 1996); George Hicks, *The Comfort Women: Japan's Brutal Regime of Enforced Prostitution in the Second World War* (New York: W.W. Norton Company, 1995); Keith Howard, *True Stories of the Korean Comfort Women* (London: Casswell, 1995); and International Commission of Jurists, *Comfort Women: An Unfinished Ordeal* (Tokyo: Akashi Shoten, 1995).

28. Brownmiller, *Against Our Will*, 70.

29. Charter of the International Military Tribunal, August 8, 1945, reprinted in Cherif Bassiouni, *Crimes Against Humanity in International Criminal Law* (The Hague: Martinus Nijhoff, 1992), 582. The charter for the Tokyo trial was substantially similar, however, the language "against any civilian population" was omitted, thereby opening the way for prosecutions for acts against military personnel. See Boling, "Mass Rape, Enforced Prostitution," 2–3.

30. Crimes against humanity have been interpreted as requiring that the acts be committed as part of a systematic attack on racial, ethnic, political, national, or religious grounds. Thus, in order to succeed with a claim that sexual abuse constitutes an "inhumane act" prohibited as a "crime against humanity," one would probably also have to argue that the act was committed as part of a systematic attack based on the grounds specified above. For a discussion of the development of these concepts, see generally Bassiouni, *Crimes Against Humanity*, and Geoffrey Best, *The Law of War Since 1945* (Oxford: Clarendon Press, 1994).

31. Under the direction of Telford Taylor as the chief prosecutor, the United States held twelve military trials at Nuremberg. For an account of these trials, see John Allan Appleman, *Military Tribunals and International Crimes* (Indianapolis, Ind.: The Bobbs-Merrill Co., 1954).

32. "Allied Control Council Law No. 10, Punishment of Persons Guilty of War Crimes, Crimes Against Peace and Humanity" (December 20, 1945) (reprinted in Bassiouni, *Crimes Against Humanity*, 590). Control Council Law 10 also specifically listed as a crime "membership in categories of a criminal group or organization declared criminal by the International Military Tribunal."

33. Bassiouni, *Crimes Against Humanity*, 125.

34. For the Nuremberg trials, see A. N. Trainin, ed., *Trial of the Major War Criminals Before the International Military Tribunal, November 14, 1945–October 1, 1946* (42 volumes, 1947) see, for example, vol. VI, transcript pages 211–14; 404–7 and vol. VII, transcript pages 449–57. For the Tokyo trials, see R. John Pritchard and Sonia Madbunua Zaide, eds., *The Tokyo War Crimes Trial: The Complete Transcripts of the Proceedings of the International Military Tribunal for the Far East* (New York: Garland Publishers, 1981), see, for example, vol. II, transcript pages 2568–73, 3904–44, 4463–79, 4526–31, 4533–36.

35. The Indictment for the Nuremberg Trial can be found at *Trial of the Major War Criminals Before the International Military Tribunal, Vol. I,* 27–68.

36. See *The Tokyo War Crimes Trial*, vol. I, transcript page 29.

37. Askin, *War Crimes Against Women*, 180.

38. Another significant human rights development of the tribunals that is not treated here included the establishment of a precedent that accused war criminals were entitled to fair trials. For more on the tribunals, see generally B. V. A. Roling, ed., *The Tokyo Trial and Beyond: Reflections of a Peacemonger* (Cambridge: Polity Press, 1993); Telford Taylor, *The Anatomy of the Nuremberg Trials: A Personal Memoir* (New York: Alfred A. Knopf, 1992); Werner Maser, *Nuremberg: A Nation on Trial* (New York: Charles Scribner's Sons, 1979); and William I. Bosch, *Judgment on Nuremberg: American Attitudes Toward the Major German War-Crime Trials* (Chapel Hill, N.C.: University of North Carolina Press, 1970).

39. See George Ginsburg and V. N. Kudriavtsev, eds., *The Nuremberg Trial and International Law* (Dordrecht: Martinus Nijhoff Publishers, 1990); and Robert K. Woetzel, *The Nuremberg Trials in International Law, with a Postlude on the Eichmann Case* (London: Stevens & Sons Unlimited, 1962).

40. Bassiouni, *Crimes Against Humanity*, 179.

41. Louis B. Sohn, "The New International Law: Protection of the Rights of Individuals Rather than States," *American University Law Review* 32 (1982), 1.

42. General Assembly Resolution 174, UN Doc A/180 (1948).

43. For a discussion of human rights and humanitarian law generally, see the companion book, *Protecting Human Rights: The Challenge to Humanitarian Organizations*, by Mark Frohardt, Diane Paul, and Larry Minear (Providence, R.I.: Watson Institute, 1999).

44. Geneva Convention for the Amelioration of the Condition of the Wounded and Sick in the Armed Forces in the Field, Aug. 12, 1949, 75 U.N.T.S. 31 (First Geneva Convention); Geneva Convention for the

Amelioration of the Condition of Wounded, Sick and Shipwrecked Members of Armed Forces at Sea, Aug. 12, 1949, 75 U.N.T.S. 85 (Second Geneva Convention); Geneva Convention Relative to the Treatment of Prisoners in War, Aug. 12, 1949, 75 U.N.T.S. 135 (Third Geneva Convention); and Geneva Convention Relative to the Protection of Civilian Persons in Time of War, Aug. 12, 1949, 75 U.N.T.S. 287 (Fourth Geneva Convention).

45. 1977 Geneva Protocol I Additional to the Geneva Conventions of 12 August 1949, and Relating to the Protection of Victims of International Armed Conflicts, Dec. 12, 1977 (Protocol I) 1125 U.N.T.S. 3; and 1977 Protocol II Additional to the Geneva Conventions of 12 August 1949, and Relating to the Protection of Victims of Non-International Armed Conflicts, Dec. 12, 1977 (Protocol II), 1125 U.N.T.S. 609.

46. See Major Thomas J. Murphy, "Sanctions and Enforcement of the Humanitarian Law of the Four Geneva Conventions of 1949 and the Geneva Protocol I of 1977," *Military Law Review* 103 (1984), 3.

47. For the importance of universal jurisdiction for cases of wartime rape, see Dorothy Q. Thomas and Regan E. Ralph, "Rape in War: Challenging the Tradition of Impunity," *SAIS Review* 14 (1994), 81, 95.

48. Fourth Geneva Convention, art. 27.

49. For analyses along this line of argument, see Evelyn Mary Aswad, "Torture by Means of Rape," *Georgetown Law Journal* 84 (1996), 1913; and Deborah Blatt, "Recognizing Rape as a Method of Torture," *New York University Review of Law and Social Change* 19 (1992), 821.

50. Convention Against Torture and Other Cruel, Inhuman, or Degrading Treatment or Punishment, Dec. 10, 1984. The definition of torture under the Torture Convention supports the proposition that rape may, under certain circumstances, constitute a form of torture. The convention defines torture in terms of three elements: (1) the intentional infliction of severe mental or physical pain or suffering; (2) by or at the instigation of or with the consent or acquiescence of a public official or any other person acting in an official capacity; (3) for one of several illicit purposes (such as obtaining a confession, punishing an act the victim is suspected to have committed, intimidating the victim or other persons, or for any reason based on discrimination of any kind).

51. Fourth Geneva Convention, articles 27 and 147.

52. See, for example, Fourth Geneva Convention, art. 3.

53. Protocol I, art. 76(1).

54. Protocol II, art. 4.

55. See Amnesty International, *The U.N. and Refugees' Human Rights: A Manual on How U.N. Human Rights Mechanisms Can Protect the Rights of Refugees* (London: Amnesty International, 1997), 48–50.

56. Francis Deng, appointed by the Secretary-General as Special Representative on Internal Displacement, wrote *Guiding Principles on Internal Displacement*. These nonbinding guidelines provide a foundation upon which the international assistance community may build in addressing the needs of the internally displaced. See Francis M. Deng, *Guiding Principles on Internal Displacement*, submitted to the Secretary-General, Feb. 11, 1998, United Nations E/CN.4/1998/53/Add. 2. Also, for a de-

tailed discussion of refugee law, see the companion book, *Protecting Human Rights: The Challenge to Humanitarian Organizations*.

57. See Nancy Kelly, "Gender-Related Persecution: Assessing the Claims of Women," *Cornell International Law Journal* 26 (1993), 625.

58. For further development of this issue, see Thomas Spikkerboer, *Women and Refugee Status: Beyond the Public/Private Distinction* (The Hague: Emancipation Council, 1994).

59. UNHCR, *Handbook on Procedures and Criteria for Determining Refugee Status Under the 1951 Convention and the 1967 Protocol Relating to the Status of Refugees*, UN Doc. HCR/PRO/4 (1979), para. 65.

60. UNHCR, *Handbook on Procedures and Criteria for Determining Refugee Status*.

61. See Deborah E. Anker, "Women Refugees: Forgotten No Longer?," *San Diego Law Review* 32 (1995), 771; Felicite Stairs and Lori Pope, "No Place Like Home: Assaulted Migrant Women's Claim to Refugee Status," *Journal of Law and Social Policy* 6 (1990), 148; A. B. Johnsson, "The International Protection of Women Refugees—A Summary of the Principal Problems and Issues," *International Journal of Refugee Law* 1 (1989), 221; and Jacqueline Greatbach, "The Gender Difference: Feminist Critiques of Refugee Discourse," *International Journal of Refugee Law* 1 (1989), 518.

62. See David Neal, "Women as a Social Group: Recognizing Sex-Based Persecution as Grounds for Asylum," *Columbia Human Rights Law Review* 20 (1988), 203 (women who face persecution because of their sex should be considered a social group under the Refugee Convention); Karen Bower, "Recognizing Violence Against Women as Persecution on the Basis of Membership in a Particular Social Group," *Georgetown Immigration Law Journal* 7 (1993), 173 (arguing that women who face violence constitute a "social group"); and Arthur Helton, "Persecution on Account of Membership in a Social Group as a Basis for Refugee Status," *Columbia Human Rights Law Review* 15 (1983), 39 (arguing for broad meaning of social group).

63. International Women's Tribune Centre et al., *Integrating Women's Human Rights into the Deliberations of the 1993 United Nations World Conference on Human Rights and into the Ongoing Work of the United Nations* (New York: International Women's Tribune Centre, 1993), 8; and Linda Cipriani, "Gender and Persecution: Protecting Women Under International Refugee Law," *Georgetown Immigration Law Journal* 7 (1993), 511, 512.

64. UNHCR, *Handbook*, paras. 77–79.

65. UNHCR, *Handbook*, paras. 77–79.

66. UNHCR, *Handbook*, para. 53.

67. UNHCR, *Handbook*, para. 54.

68. Audrey Macklin, "Refugee Women and the Imperative of Categories," *Human Rights Quarterly* 17 (1995), 213.

69. James C. Hathaway, *The Law of Refugee Status* (Toronto: Butterworths, 1991), 135–36.

70. Resolution on the Application of the Geneva Convention relating to the Status of Refugees, 1984 O.J. (C127) 137. The same year the Dutch

Refugee Council similarly recognized gender-based claims of persecution: "It is the opinion of the Dutch Refugee Council that persecution for reason of membership in a particular social group may also be taken to include persecution because of social position on the basis of sex. This may be especially true in situations where discrimination against women in society, contrary to the rulings in international law, has been institutionalized and where women who oppose this discrimination or distance themselves from it are faced with drastic sanctions, either from the authorities themselves, or from their social environment, where the authorities are unwilling or unable to offer protection." Macklin, "Refugee Women and the Imperative of Categories," 216, n. 12.

71. UNHCR, *Refugee Women and International Protection*, para. 205, UN Doc. A/AG.96/673 (1985).

72. UNHCR, *Refugee Women and International Protection*, para. 115(4) (K).

73. "Report of the International Consultation on Refugee Women, Geneva, November 15–19, 1988, With Particular Reference to Protection Problems," *International Journal of Refugee Law* 1 (1989), 233.

74. "Report of the International Consultation on Refugee Women," para. 236.

75. UNHCR, *Report of the United Nations High Commissioner for Refugees Executive Committee, 39th Sess.*, UN Doc. A/AC.96/721 (1988).

76. See "Making the Linkages: Protection and Assistance Policy and Programming to Benefit Refugee Women," UN ESCOR, Executive Comm. of the High Commissioner's Programme, UN Doc. E/CN.6/SC.2/CRP.16 (1993).

77. *CSW Report on Refugee and Displaced Women and Children*, UN ESCOR, Commission on the Status of Women, 35th Sess., Agenda Item 5c, UN Doc. E/CN.6/1991/4 (1990).

78. UNHCR Policy on Refugee Women, *Report of the United Nations High Commissioner for Refugees Executive Committee, 41st Sess.*, UN Doc. A/AC.96/754 (1990).

79. Conclusions on the International Protection of Refugees, Conclusion No. 560 (XL), UN HCR, Executive Committee of the High Commissioner's Programme, UN Doc. HCR/IP/2 (1989).

80. UNHCR Executive Committee, *Note on Refugee Women and International Protection*, EC/SCP/59 (August 28, 1990), at 5.

81. UNHCR, *Guidelines for the Protection of Refugee Women*, UN Doc. ES/SCP/67 (1991).

82. UNHCR, *Guidelines for the Protection of Refugee Women* at 9, paras. 9–10.

83. Interview with Susan Forbes Martin, Washington D.C., 1998.

84. UNHCR, *Sexual Violence against Women: Guidelines on Prevention and Response* (Geneva: UNHCR, 1995).

85. See Human Rights Watch, *Discussion Paper: Protection in the Decade of Voluntary Repatriation*, September 20, 1996.

86. Mary Anderson et al., *A Framework for People-Oriented Planning in Refugee Situations Taking Account of Women, Men and Children* (Geneva: UNHCR, December 1992) .

87. *A Framework for People-Oriented Planning*, 1.
88. Mary Anderson et al., *People-Oriented Planning at Work: Using POP to Improve UNHCR Programming* (Geneva: UNHCR, 1992).
89. UNHCR, *An Inter-Agency Field Manual: Reproductive Health in Refugee Situations* (Geneva: UNHCR, 1995).
90. UNHCR, World Health Organization and the Joint United Nations Programme on HIV/AIDs (UNAIDS), *Guidelines for HIV Interventions in Emergency Settings* (Geneva: UNHCR, 1996).
91. See Judy A. Benjamin and Khadija Fancy, *The Gender Dimensions of Internal Displacement: Concept Paper and Annotated Bibliography*. Submitted to the Office of Emergency Programmes, UNICEF by the Women's Commission for Refugee Women and Children, September 1998.
92. UNHCR, *Guidelines on the Protection of Refugee Women*, 9, para. 8.
93. UNHCR, *Guidelines on the Protection of Refugee Women*, 9, para. 8.
94. Immigration and Refugee Board, *Guidelines Issued by the Chairperson Pursuant to Section 65(3) of the Immigration Act: Women Refugee Claimants Fearing Gender-Related Persecution* (1993) [hereafter *Canadian Guidelines*].
95. *Canadian Guidelines*, 6.
96. *Canadian Guidelines*, 7.
97. *Canadian Guidelines*, 2. See also Kristine M. Fox, "Gender Persecution: Canadian Guidelines Offer a Model for Refugee Determination in the United States," *Arizona Journal of International and Comparative Law* 11 (1994), 117.
98. Immigration and Naturalization Service, "Consideration for Asylum Officers Adjudicating Asylum Claims from Women" (1995) [hereafter "U.S. Consideration"].
99. "U.S. Consideration," 9.
100. "U.S. Consideration," 9.
101. "U.S. Consideration," 9.
102. Article 55 of the Charter for the United Nations states that the UN shall promote the "universal respect for, and observance of, human rights and fundamental freedoms for all without distinction as to race, sex, language or religion." UN Charter, June 26, 1945, 59 Stat. 1031, U.S.T.S. No. 993.
103. General Assembly Resolution 217, UN GAO, 3rd Sess., UN Doc. A/810, (1948), art. 14.
104. General Assembly Resolution 2200, UN GAO, 21st Sess., Supp. No. 16 at 52, UN Doc. A/6316 (1967), art. 3.
105. General Assembly Resolution 2200, UN GAO, 21st Sess., Supp. No. 16, at 49, UN Doc. A/6316 (1967), art. 3.
106. Convention to Eliminate All Forms of Discrimination Against Women, Dec. 18, 1979, 19 I.L.M. 33.
107. Convention to Eliminate All Forms of Discrimination Against Women, 8, para. 7.
108. Convention on the Rights of the Child, adopted by the General Assembly on 20 November 1989, entered into force 2 September 1990.
109. UNHCR, *Guidelines on the Protection of Refugee Women*, 8.
110. See Women, Law & Development International and Human Rights

Watch, Women's Rights Project, *Women's Human Rights Step by Step* (Washington, D.C.: Women, Law, and Development, 1997), 122.

111. WHO/UNICEF/UNFPA Joint Statement, February 1996 (as quoted in Amnesty International), *1998: A Wonderful Year for Women's Human Rights?* AI Index: IOR 40/12/97 (January 14, 1998).

112. See *DAW Report*.

113. UN, "Declaration on the Protection of Women and Children in Emergency and Armed Conflict," General Assembly Resolution 3318 (XXIX), 14 December 1974.

114. *DAW Report*, 5.

115. UN, *Report of the World Conference to Review and Appraise the Achievements of the United Nations Decade for Women: Equality, Development and Peace*, A/CONF.116/28/Rev.1, 1986, para. 41.

116. Security Council Resolution 798 of December 1992.

117. Declaration on the Elimination of Violence against Women, UN ESCOR, Commission on the Status of Women, Annex I, UN Doc. E/CN.6/WG.2/ 1992/L.3 (1992) adopted July 27, 1993, UN ESCOR, UN Doc. A/C.3/ 48/L.5 (1993).

118. Declaration on the Elimination of Violence against Women, at Article 1.

119. Declaration on the Elimination of Violence against Women.

120. See, for example, United Nations, *Preliminary Report Submitted by the Special Rapporteur on Violence Against Women, Its Causes and Consequences*, UN Doc. E/CN.4/1995/42 (1994), paras. 288 and 290.

121. Amnesty International, *The U.N. and Refugees' Human Rights: A Manual on How U.N. Human Rights Mechanisms Can Protect the Rights of Refugees* (London: Amnesty International, 1997), 30.

122. UN, *Preliminary Report of the Special Rapporteur on the Situation of Systematic Rape, Sexual Slavery and Slavery-Like Practices During Periods of Armed Conflict*, E/CN.4/Sub.2/1996/26, 16 July 1996.

123. UN, *Working Paper on the Situation of Systematic Rape, Sexual Slavery and Slavery-Like Practices During Warfare, Including Internal Armed Conflict*, E/CN.4/Sub.2/1995/38, 13 July 1995.

124. UN, *Preparatory Document on the Question of Systematic Rape, Sexual Slavery and Slavery-Like Practices During Wartime*, E/CN.4/Sub.2/1993/ 447, 7 Sept. 1993.

125. See CHR Res. 1997/37 (April 11, 1997), inviting thematic special rapporteurs and working groups to "include regularly in their reports gender-disaggregated data and to address the characteristics and practice of human rights violations under their mandate that are specifically or primarily directed against women, or to which women are particularly vulnerable, in order to ensure effective protection of their human rights."

126. Grave breaches include the following acts against persons or property protected under the provisions of the relevant Geneva Convention:
(a) willful killing;
(b) torture or inhumane treatment, including biological experiments;
(c) willfully causing great suffering or serious injury to body or health;
(d) extensive destruction and appropriation of property, not justified by military necessity and carried out unlawfully and wantonly;

(e) compelling a prisoner of war or a civilian to serve in the forces of a hostile power;

(f) willfully depriving a prisoner of war or a civilian of the rights of a fair and regular trial;

(g) unlawful deportation or transfer or unlawful confinement of a civilian; and

(h) taking civilians as hostages.

127.  Genocide means any of the following acts committed with intent to destroy, in whole or in part, a national, ethnical, racial or religious group, as such:

(a) killing members of the group;

(b) causing serious bodily or mental harm to members of the group;

(c) deliberately inflicting on the group conditions of life calculated to bring about its physical destruction in whole or in part;

(d) imposing measures intended to prevent births within the group; and

(e) forcibly transferring children of one group to another.

128.  Crimes against humanity include the following crimes "directed against any civilian population: (a) murder; (b) extermination; (c)enslavement; (d) deportation; (e) imprisonment; (f) torture; (g) rape; (h) persecution on political, racial and religious grounds; and (i) other inhumane acts."

129.  Inter-American Convention on the Prevention, Punishment and Eradication of Violence Against Women, June 9, 1994, reprinted in *International Human Rights Reports* 3 (1996), 232.

130.  United Nations, *Report of the Fourth World Conference on Women Held in Beijing from 4 to 15 September 1995, Including the Agenda, the Beijing Declaration and the Platform for Action*, A/Conf.177/20, 17 October 1995 (hereafter "Beijing Platform for Action"). See also GA Res. 50/203, UN GOAR, 50th Sess., Supp. No. 49, Vol. 1, at 270, UN Doc. A/50/49 (1995).

131.  *Beijing Platform for Action*, para. 124(r).

132.  *Beijing Platform for Action*, para. 133.

133.  *Beijing Platform for Action*, para. 135.

134.  *Beijing Platform for Action*, para. 136.

135.  *Beijing Platform for Action*, para. 137.

## Chapter 4

1.  Robert Casson and Associates, *Does Aid Work?* 2nd ed. (Oxford: Clarendon Press, 1994), 92.

2.  Casson and Associates, *Does Aid Work?*, 92. See CIDA, *Women in Development: Policy Framework* (Ottawa: CIDA, 1984).

3.  Lutheran World Relief Statement on Gender Equity (not dated, but accompanied by cover letter dated August 8, 1996).

4.  Information on this section is taken from a nomination form for an award from InterAction to LWR for gender efforts and from interviews with LWR staff.

5.  Lutheran World Relief, Gender Packet (as revised August 12, 1997). Includes gender timetable, LWR response to InterAction gender survey, Counterpart Agency Gender Survey, and suggestions for further resources.

6. This tool was drawn from three other models: from USAID's Gensys Project, InterAction, and Center for Development and Population Activities (CEDPA).

7. Other steps taken by LWR on gender issues include creation of an ongoing electronic dialogue on gender issues, regional workshops and training, and publications on gender and development. One example of a local LWR program on gender was the "networking gender and development" program launched in the Philippines. This program worked primarily through continual gender sessions/trainings with people's organizations and through implementation of gender issues in agrarian projects. Local leaders were very much involved.

8. See Catholic Relief Services (CRS), "Gender Responsive Programming" (policy statement endorsed at the end of November 1997). One of the reasons for the progress of CRS and LWR on gender issues appears to be strong and dedicated boards of directors and personnel at all levels who hold a sincere interest in promoting gender equity. LWR draws its inspiration from a social change and social justice movement that holds equality and equity as basic tenets, and CRS builds on a broad concept of justice from Catholic social teaching.

9. Karen Mussalo, et al., *Refugee Law and Policy* (Durham, N.C.: Carolina Academic Press, 1997), 601.

10. See Swedish International Development Cooperation Agency (Sida), *Overview: Gender Equality and Emergency Assistance/Conflict Resolution* (Stockholm: Sida, 1997), 1.

11. Mary Anderson, *Focusing on Women: UNIFEM's Experience in Mainstreaming* (New York: UNIFEM, 1993), 5. The concept of mainstreaming gender or women's concerns has been applied to the human rights system generally. At its fifty-second session, in 1996, the Commission on Human Rights called for the intensified effort at the international level to mainstream the rights of women into United Nations systemwide activity. See Commission on Human Rights, Fifty-Third Session, Item 9 on the provisional agenda, "Integrating the Human Rights of Women Throughout the United Nations System," E/CN.4/1997/40 (December 20, 1996). For a status report on mainstreaming human rights throughout the UN system, see Karen Kenny, *When Needs Are Rights: An Overview of UN Efforts to Integrate Human Rights in Humanitarian Action* (Providence, R.I.: Watson Institute, 2000).

12. Office of the Special Adviser on Gender Issues and Advancement of Women, "Report of the United Nations Intragency Gender Mission to Afghanistan" (November 12–24, 1997), 11.

13. For a good listing of specific assistance and protection actions related to women, see League of Red Cross and Red Crescent Societies, *Working with Women in Emergency Relief and Rehabilitation Programmes*, Field Studies Paper No. 2 (May 1991).

14. Good examples of such a partnering approach can be found in Chiapas. See Itziar Lozano, *Lessons Learned in Work with Refugee Women: A Case Study of Chiapas*, report for UNHCR, Sub-Office (Comitan, Chiapas, Mexico, 1996).

15. See, for example, International Federation of Red Cross and Red Crescent

Societies, "Women's Role in Red Cross and Red Crescent Societies" (Geneva: ICRC, undated) [Internal audit undertaken as preparation for Beijing Conference].

16. This example was provided by Susan Forbes Martin, Washington, D.C., December 1997.

17. See 1997 Women's Commission Project.

18. Hlmira Etemodi, coordinator of the International Working Group on Refugee Women, Geneva, June 1998.

19. Myriam Tebouri, United Nations Officer, Center for Human Rights, Geneva, June 1998.

20. Women's Commission Project, 7.

# ABBREVIATIONS

| | |
|---|---|
| ACBAR | Agency Coordinating Body for Afghan Relief |
| BWI | Bosnian Women's Initiative |
| CAGS | Counterpart Agency Gender Study (LWR) |
| CEDAW | Convention on the Elimination of All Forms of Discrimination Against Women (also known as The Women's Convention) |
| CEDPA | Center for Development and Population Activities |
| CIDA | Canadian International Development Agency |
| CRC | Committee on the Rights of the Child (UN) |
| CRS | Catholic Relief Services |
| CSW | Commission on the Status of Women (UN) |
| DAW | Division for the Advancement of Women (UN Secretariat) |
| DFID | Department for International Development (UK) |
| EC | European Community |
| ECHO | European Community Humanitarian Office |
| FGM | Female Genital Mutilation |
| FRY | Federal Republic of Yugoslavia |
| IAM | International Assistance Mission |
| ICCPR | International Covenant on Civil and Political Rights |
| ICESCR | International Covenant on Social, Economic and Cultural Rights |
| ICRC | International Committee of the Red Cross |
| ICTY | International Criminal Tribunal for the former Yugoslavia |
| IDP | Internally displaced person |
| IFRC | International Federation of Red Cross and Red Crescent Societies |
| IMF | International Monetary Fund |
| INS | Immigration and Naturalization Service (US) |
| IOM | International Organization for Migration |

| | |
|---|---|
| IRC | International Rescue Committee |
| KLA | Kosovo Liberation Army |
| LWR | Lutheran World Relief |
| MSF | Médicins sans Frontières (Doctors Without Borders) |
| NATO | North Atlantic Treaty Organization |
| NGO | Nongovernmental organization |
| OCHA | Office for the Coordination of Humanitarian Affairs (UN) |
| OSCE | Organization for Security and Cooperation in Europe |
| PDPA | Peoples' Democratic Party of Afghanistan |
| POP | People-Oriented Programming (UNHCR) |
| SFA | Strategic Framework Approach (UN) |
| UDHR | Universal Declaration of Human Rights |
| UN | United Nations |
| UNDP | United Nations Development Programme |
| UNFPA | United Nations Fund for Population Activities |
| UNHCR | United Nations High Commissioner for Refugees |
| UNICEF | United Nations Children's Fund |
| UNIFEM | United Nations Development Fund for Women |
| UNPROFOR | United Nations Protection Force |
| USAID | United States Agency for International Development |
| WFP | World Food Programme (UN) |
| WHO | World Health Organization (UN) |

# BIBLIOGRAPHY

Adjin-Tettey, Elizabeth. "Failure of State Protection Within the Context of the Convention Refuge Regime with Particular Reference to Gender-Related Persecution." *Journal of International Legal Studies* 3 (1997), 53.

Agger, Inger. Mary Bille, trans. *The Blue Room: Trauma and Testimony Among Refugee Women: A Psychosocial Exploration*. London: Zed Books, 1994.

America's Watch and Women's Rights Project. *Untold Terror: Violence Against Women in Peru's Armed Conflict*. New York: Human Rights Watch, 1992.

Anderson, Mary, et al. *People-Oriented Planning at Work: Using POP to Improve UNHCR Programming*. Geneva: UNHCR, December 1992.

Anker, Deborah E. "Women Refugees: Forgotten No Longer?" *San Diego Law Review* 32 (1995), 771.

Askin, Kelly Dawn. *War Crimes Against Women: Prosecution in International Tribunals*. The Hague: Martinus Nijhoff Publishers, 1997.

Bartsch, Jonathan. "CARE Afghanistan Case Study: Violent Conflict and Human Rights: A Study of Principled Decision Making in Afghanistan." CARE Internal Report (October 1998).

Blatt, Deborah. "Recognizing Rape as a Method of Torture." *New York University Review of Law and Social Change* 19 (1992), 821.

Bonnerjea, Lucy. *Shaming the World: The Needs of Women Refugees*. London: Change, 1985.

Cammack, Diana. "Gender Relief and Politics During the Afghan War." In *Engendering Forced Migration: Theory and Practice*, edited by Doreen Indra, *Refugee and Forced Migration Studies, vol. 5*. New York: Berghahn Books, 1999.

Cipriani, Linda. "Gender and Persecution: Protecting Women Under

International Refugee Law." *Georgetown Immigration Law Journal* 7 (1993), 511.

Cohen, Roberta. *Refugee and Internally Displaced Women: A Development Perspective.* Washington, D.C.: The Brookings Institution, 1995.

Cole, Ellen, Olivia M. Espin, and Esther D. Rothblum, eds. *Refugee Women and Their Mental Health: Shattered Societies, Shattered Lives.* New York: Hawthorn Press, 1992.

Commission on Human Rights, Report of the Special Rapporteur on Violence Against Women, UN Doc. E/CN.4/1998/54/Add.1, 4 February 1998.

Deng, Francis and Roberta Cohen. *Masses in Flight : The Global Crisis of Internal Displacement.* Washington D.C.: The Brookings Institution, 1988.

El-Bushra, Judy and Cecile Mukarubuga. "Women, War and Transition." *Gender and Development* 3, no. 3 (1995), 16.

El-Bushra, Judy and Eugenia Pia Lopes. "The Gender of Armed Conflict." In *Development and Conflict: The Gender Dimension.* Oxford: Oxfam, 1994, 18.

Frohardt, Mark, Diane Paul, and Larry Minear. *Protecting Human Rights: The Challenge to Humanitarian Organizations.* Occasional Paper #35. Providence, R.I.: Watson Institute, 1999.

Girardet, Edward and Jonathan Walter, eds. *Essential Field Guides to Humanitarian and Conflict Zones: Afghanistan.* Geneva and Dublin: Crosslines Communications, Ltd. and International Centre for Humanitarian Reporting, 1998.

Goodhand, Jonathan with Peter Chamberlain. "'Dancing with the Prince': NGOs' Survival Strategies in the Afghan Conflict." *Development in Practice* vol. 6, no. 3 (1996).

Greatbach, Jacqueline. "The Gender Difference: Feminist Critiques of Refugee Discourse." *International Journal of Refugee Law* 1 (1989), 518.

Human Rights Watch (Africa Watch and Women's Rights Project). "Seeking Refuge, Finding Terror: The Widespread Rape of Somali Women Refugees in North Eastern Kenya." *A Human Rights Watch Short Report* 5, no. 13 (October 1993).

Human Rights Watch (Africa Watch and Women's Rights Project). *Shattered Lives: Sexual Violence During the Rwandan Genocide and its Aftermath.* New York: Human Rights Watch, 1996.

International Commission of Jurists. *Comfort Women: An Unfinished Ordeal.* Tokyo: Akashi Shoten, 1995.

Kenny, Karen. *When Needs Are Rights: An Overview of UN Efforts to Integrate Human Rights in Humanitarian Action.* Occasional Paper #38. Providence, R.I.: Watson Institute, 2000.

Lang, Erica and Eimad Mahanna. *A Study of Women and Work in Shatti Refugee Camp of the Gaza Strip.* Jerusalem: Arab Thought Forum, 1992.

League of Red Cross and Red Crescent Societies. "Working With Women in Emergency Relief and Rehabilitation Programmes." Field Studies Paper No. 2 (May 1991).

Le Duc, Carol and Homa Sabri. "Room to Manoeuvre: Study of Women's Programming In Afghanistan." Report prepared for UNDP/ Kabul, Islamabad, 1996.

Macklin, Audrey. "Refugee Women and the Imperative of Categories." *Human Rights Quarterly* 17 (1995), 213.

Magnus, Ralph H. and Eden Naby. *Afghanistan Mullah, Marx, and Mujahidin.* Boulder, Colo.: Westview Press, 1998.

Malone, Linda A. "Beyond Bosnia and In Re Kasinga: A Feminist Perspective on Recent Developments in Protecting Women from Sexual Violence." *Boston University International Law Journal* 14 (1996), 319.

Marin, Leni and Blandina Lansang-de Mesa, eds. *Women on the Move: Proceedings of Workshop on Human Rights Abuses Against Immigrant & Refugee Women.* London: Family Violence Prevention Fund, 1993.

Marsden, Peter. *The Taliban: War, Religion and the New Order in Afghanistan.* London: Zed Books Ltd., 1999.

Martin, Susan Forbes. *Refugee Women.* London: Zed Books, 1992.

Mayotte, Judith A. *Disposable People? The Plight of Refugees.* Maryknoll, N.Y.: Orbis Books, 1992.

Mertus, Julie. *Kosovo: How Myths and Truths Started a War.* Berkeley: University of California, 1999.

Mertus, Julie. *Internal Displacement in Kosovo: The Impact on Women and Children: A Field Report Assessing the Emergency and Making Recommendations on an Effective Humanitarian Response.* New York: Women's Commission for Refugee Women and Children, June 1998.

Mertus, Julie. "The State and the Post-Cold War Refugee Regime: New Models, New Questions." *International Journal of Refugee Law* 10, no. 3 (1998), 321–48.

Mertus, Julie, ed. et al. *The Suitcase: Refugee Voices from Bosnia and Croatia.* Berkeley: University of California Press, 1997.

Mertus, Julie with Nancy Flowers and Mallika Dutt. *Local Action/Global Change: Learning About the Human Rights of Women and Girls.* New York: UNIFEM and the Center for Women's Global Leadership, 1999.

Middleton, Neil and Phil O'Keefe. *Disaster and Development: The Politics of Humanitarian Aid.* London: Pluto Press, 1998.

O'Neill, William G. *A Humanitarian Practitioner's Guide to International Human Rights Law.* Occasional Paper #34. Providence, R.I.: Watson Institute, 1999.

Nef, C. E. J. de and S. J. de Ruiter. *Sexual Violence Against Women Refugees.* The Hague: Ministry for Social Affairs, 1984.

Pont, Anna M. "'Eat What You Want, Dress the Way Your Community Wants'—The Position of Afghan Women in MCI Programme Areas." Seattle: Mercy Corps International, 1998.

Ralph, Regan. "Mapping Gender Violence" [an editorial]. *Relief and Rehabilitation Newsletter*, no. 14 (June 1999).

Report of the Secretary-General, United Nations Commission on the Status of Women, "Peace: Refugee and Displaced Women and Children," UN Doc. E/CN.6/1991/4, Vienna (November 9, 1990).

Report of the Secretary-General, Commission on Human Rights, "Integrating the Human Rights of Women Throughout the United Nations System," UN Doc. E/CN.4/1997/40 (20 December 1996).

Rubin, Barnett R. *The Fragmentation of Afghanistan: State Formation and Collapse in the International System.* New Haven, Conn.: Yale University Press, 1995.

Spikkerboer, Thomas. *Women and Refugee Status: Beyond the Public/Private Distinction.* The Hague: Emancipation Council, 1994.

Seifert, Ruth. *War and Rape: Analytical Approaches.* Geneva: Women's International League for Peace and Freedom, 1993.

Swedish International Development Cooperation Agency (Sida). *Overview: Gender Equality and Emergency Assistance/Conflict Resolution.* Stockholm: Sida, 1997.

Swiss, Shana and Joan E. Giller. "Rape as a Crime of War: A Medical Perspective." *JAMA* 270 (1993), 613.

United Nations Division for the Advancement of Women. "Sexual Violence and Armed Conflict: United Nations Responses." *Women 2000* (April 1998).

United Nations Office of the Special Adviser on Gender Issues and Advancement of Women. "Report of the United Nations Inter-Agency Gender Mission to Afghanistan." New York, November 12–24, 1997.

United Nations. *Working Paper on the Situation of Systematic Rape,*

*Sexual Slavery and Slavery-Like Practices During Warfare, Including Internal Armed Conflict.* E/CN.4/Sub.2/1995/38, 13 July 1995.

UNHCR. *An Inter-Agency Field Manual: Reproductive Health in Refugee Situations.* Geneva: UNHCR, 1995.

UNHCR. *Guidelines for the Protection of Refugee Women.* UN Doc. ES/SCP/67 (1991).

UNHCR. *Refugee Women and UNHCR: Implementing the Beijing Platform for Action.* Geneva: UNHCR, 1998.

Walsh, Martha. "Where Feminist Theory Failed to Meet Development Practice—A Missed Opportunity in Bosnia and Herzegovina." *The European Journal of Women's Studies 5.* London: Sage Publications, 1998, 329–43.

Werntz, Mary. "Women & the Reconstruction Process in Afghanistan: The UNDP/OPS Women's Livestock Projects." Master's thesis. Cornell University (1997).

Women, Law, and Development and Human Rights Watch (Women's Rights Project). *Women's Human Rights Step by Step.* Washington, D.C.: Women, Law, and Development and Human Rights Watch, 1997.

Woroniuk, Beth, et al. *Overview: Gender Equality and Emergency Assistance/Conflict Resolution.* Stockholm: Swedish International Development Cooperation Agency, January 1997.

# INDEX

# ABOUT THE AUTHORS

JULIE A. MERTUS is an assistant professor in the Department of International Peace and Conflict Resolution in the School of International Service, American University. During 2000–2001, a senior fellow at the U.S. Institute of Peace. A graduate of Yale Law School, she was formerly a fellow in human rights at Harvard Law School, a Fulbright professor in Romania, a MacArthur Foundation fellow, and an attorney with Human Rights Watch.

Her books include *Kosovo: How Myths and Truths Started a War* (University of California Press, 1999); *Local Action/Global Change: Learning About the Human Rights of Women and Girls* (UNIFEM and the Center for Women's Global Leadership, 1999) with Nancy Flowers and Mallika Dutt; and *The Suitcase: Refugee Voices from Bosnia and Croatia* (University of California Press, 1997) (co-editor). She serves as a consultant to a variety of humanitarian and human rights organizations, nongovernmental and UN alike.

JUDY A. BENJAMIN directs the Protection and Participation Project of the Women's Commission for Refugee Women and Children. She provides expert consultation to NGOs, the United Nations, and government agencies on the impact of war on women. Her contributions to mainstreaming gender in international assistance include a gender review of the Sphere Project's Humanitarian Charter and Minimum Standards in Disaster Response and participation in a review of the *Guiding Principles on Internal Displacement* to ensure appropriate gender language. She researched and wrote *The Gender Dimensions of Internal Displacement* with Khadjia Fancy for a joint UNICEF/Women's Commission endeavor. She contributed to the development of the first edition of the UNHCR *Field Manual for Reproductive Health*.

She is a Ph.D. candidate at Binghamton University. Her work in Afghanistan began in early 1997, when she provided technical gender advice to NGOs operating in Afghanistan.

# THE HUMANITARIANISM AND WAR PROJECT

THE HUMANITARIANISM AND WAR PROJECT is an independent policy research initiative underwritten by some fifty UN agencies, governments, NGOs, and foundations. Since its inception in 1991, it has conducted thousands of interviews in and about complex emergencies around the world, producing an array of case studies, handbooks and training materials, articles, and opinion pieces for a diverse audience of humanitarian practitioners, policy analysts, academics, and the general public.

During the years 1997–2000, the Project has been examining the process of institutional learning and change among humanitarian organizations in the post–Cold War period. Recognizing that humanitarian agencies are nowadays not only in greater demand but are also experiencing greater difficulty in carrying out their tasks, the Project is highlighting innovative practices to address specific challenges. Beginning in 2000 it will step up its efforts to disseminate its findings and recommendations.

Following earlier residence at the Refugee Policy Group in Washington, D.C. and at the Thomas J. Watson Jr. Institute for International Studies, the Project is now located at the Feinstein International Famine Center at Tufts University's School of Nutrition and Science Policy. A detailed list of its contributors and publications is available at the website below.

The Humanitarianism and War Project
Feinstein International Famine Center
Tufts University
96 Packard Avenue
Medford, MA 02155
(617) 627-3423
e-mail: h&w@tufts.edu
www.hwproject.tufts.edu